HANDS ON FEET

The New System that Makes Reflexology a Snap!

by Michelle R. Kluck

RUNNING PRESS
PHILADELPHIA · LONDON

9   8   7   6   5   4   3   2   1

Digit on the right indicates the number of this printing
Library of Congress Cataloging-in-Publication Number 00-134987

ISBN 0-7624-0961-4

Cover illustration by Sheila Smallwood
Cover photo by David Safian
Interior design by Mary Ann Liquori
Interior illustrations by Carolyn Reyes
Edited by Nancy Armstrong and Jason Rekulak
Typography: Cheltenham and Berkeley

This book may be ordered by mail from the publisher.
Please include $2.50 for postage and handling.
But try your bookstore first!

Running Press Book Publishers
125 South Twenty-second Street
Philadelphia, Pennsylvania 19103-4399

Visit us on the web!
www.runningpress.com

TO MOM AND DAD

ACKNOWLEDGEMENTS

I am tremendously grateful to have so many wonderful people in my life and I wish I could personally thank everyone for helping me learn and grow throughout the years. It would be impossible to thank them all, but I would like to express my gratitude to the following people for giving me encouragement and support in writing this book. First and foremost, thank you to John Brown, who endured the whole process with patience and love. You will always be in my heart. To my parents, Richard and Helen Kluck, and Cheryl and Ahmer Nizam, who opened their homes for my refuge. To Carmen and Jack Kazan for their love and support. And a special thanks to Char Margolis, who literally walked me through many years and gave me the encouragement and love to pursue all of my dreams.

To my childhood friends and soulmates, Robert Teichert, Lauren Mencis, and Christine Thelmo, thank you for always being there for me. Thanks also to my brilliant girlfriends, Sheila Smallwood and Carolyn Reyes. My deep gratitude to Jack Ashton, who encouraged me to take that first massage class, and to Jim Reach, whose advice and help with the Sox™ was invaluable, and to Joni Eccleston, who helped organized and strengthen Basic Knead. I am forever grateful for the generosity, support, and good advice of Phil Joe, Chiwai Eng, Terren Peizer, and Scott Bader. Much love to my LA girlfriends Christine Balling, JJ Caruth, and Jacquelyn Overcash.

A special thanks to my fabulous publicist, Lisa Elia, and to everyone at Living Arts who gave me the opportunity to create products that will help people bring massage into their daily lives.

I would like to extend my deepest appreciation and thanks to Jennie Dunham, my literary agent, who believed in this project from the very beginning and brought it to life. Thanks also to Trish Telesco, for her precious advice, expertise, and creativity. My gratitude to Jennifer Worick, Jason Rekulak, Nancy Armstrong, and everyone at Running Press Book Publishers.

Finally, I would like to thank all my clients throughout the years, whose energy and supportive feedback have given me the confidence to expand and transform my massage practice. I learned something from every single one of you, and I am eternally grateful for the opportunity to share your energy and touch your life.

TABLE OF CONTENTS

Introduction

"THE PAVED HIGHWAY OF BELIEF THROUGH TOUCH
AND SIGHT LEADS STRAIGHTEST INTO THE HUMAN HEART
AND THE PRECINCTS OF THE MIND."

Lucretius

After working on hundreds of different feet, in all shapes and sizes, I have come to realize that nearly everyone loves to have their feet stroked, kneaded, stretched, and just simply touched. With over 7,000 nerves connecting the feet to the rest of the body, the incredible sensation that you feel when someone touches your feet in a caring and compassionate way can relax and de-stress your body, mind, and soul. Oftentimes, the second I place my hands on someone's feet, I can feel his body melt as every muscle lets go. As I stroke each foot, his face relaxes, his eyes close, and he drifts away to a peaceful state of bliss. Once you've experienced this feeling, you're hooked.

Throughout my practice as a massage therapist, my clients have always asked me questions about why some areas of their feet hurt more than others, and why they feel so good after their feet are massaged. After I explain the ABC's of reflexology and how a specific part of the body is related to the tender areas on their feet, most clients are so fascinated that they want to know more. Usually, this leads to them telling me about every ache and pain in their body, with the hopes that I might direct them to exactly where on their feet these aches and pains are connect-ed. After explaining how reflexology works and the location of the reflex points so many times to my clients, I decided to create a sock that would make it easy for them to understand the fundamentals of reflexology.

In 1999, I created Reflexology Sox™, a pair of unisex, one-size-fits-all socks with a unique design on the sole showing the reflex areas that correspond with specific body parts. My intention was to use the Reflexology Sox™ as an instructional tool that could help answer many of the questions that my clients asked while I massaged their feet. Also, I wanted to create a product that would encourage people to learn self-massage techniques on their feet, so that they could relieve many common problems that they might experience and not have to rely solely on treatments from me. Since many of my clients travel frequently, I thought that the Reflexology Sox™ would be a great, easy-to-pack item that they could take everywhere—even on airplanes—to alleviate stress and relax the body and mind.

I know that "touch" is essential to maintaining overall good health. I also know that "touch" is one of the most neglected senses and is seriously lacking in today's fast-paced society. One of the most important reasons I created the Reflexology Sox™ and am now writing this book is to encourage and teach people to bring "touch" into their daily lives. While I highly recommend that everyone learn a few simple massage techniques for the body, I believe that the feet are the most significant part of the body to learn to touch for two reasons: First, by stimulating the soles of the feet you can affect the entire body, and second, the foot is a part of the body that is hardly ever touched.

My hope is that this book will encourage many people to learn the simple yet invaluable techniques of reflexology and use their own touch to relieve stress in themselves and others. While I don't believe that it should be used as a substitute for conventional medical treatment, I believe that reflexology can conquer many health problems naturally, and can also serve as a form of preventative maintenance. It's a safe, easy, and beneficial method of treatment that can help you take responsibility and control of your own health. Reflexology can heighten your own body awareness and help you realize the connection between your body, mind, and spirit. So take off those shoes and pay some attention to your soles!

Chapter 1:
The Sole Story

"HEAVEN IS UNDER OUR FEET AS WELL AS OVER OUR HEADS."

Henry David Thoreau

PART I:
THE HIS-TOE-RY OF REFLEXOLOGY

ANCIENT HIS-TOE-RY OF REFLEXOLOGY

Although it has recently become a popular and accepted form of alternative therapy here in the West, reflexology has been around for a very long time. No one really knows how old reflexology is, although there is substantial evidence to suggest that it may have been used as long ago as 5,000 years. The art of reflexology appears in several forms among many ancient cultures including Egypt, China, Russia, and Japan. In these and other settings, manipulating the feet to restore balance to the body was a recognized healing technique. Some experts believe that reflexology in a more familiar form dates back to the Fourth Century B.C., when it originated alongside the ancient Oriental practices of shiatsu and acupuncture. North American Indian medicine men manipulated and stimulated the feet as a part of their healing practices, too!

The most concrete evidence of the practice of reflexology in ancient culture was the discovery of a wall painting in the tomb of Ankhmahor, "The Tomb of the Physician," located in Saqqara, an ancient burial ground of Egyptian pharaohs. This Egyptian wall painting was dated 2330 B.C., and showed hand and foot reflexology. Another example of Egyptian footwork is a pictograph of soldiers having their feet tended on a military campaign during the battle of Qadesh during the reign of Rameses II.

It seems that the ancient Egyptians were very much a "barefoot society," and these pictographs show the attention that they paid to their feet. More importantly for the evolution of modern reflexology, the Egyptians believed that the human body was a symphony of vibrations, and that the internal organs form an intricate orchestra. They also believed that these organs could be "played" by manipulating points on the feet.

More evidence of the ancient practice of reflexology is a statement by the Roman emperor Octavian, who noted that Mark Anthony rubbed Cleopatra's feet at dinner parties: "Due to his 'pathetic enslavement to her [Cleopatra]'... [Mark Anthony] even massaged her feet at dinner parties." Cleopatra lived from 69 B.C. to 30 B.C.; this statement about a public display of foot massage indicates that a reverence toward feet may have spanned the whole of ancient Egyptian civilization.

Throughout Asia, several examples of ancient foot therapies remain for our examination. In the Medicine Teacher Temple in Nara, Japan, there is a stone carving that depicts "Buddha's footprints," or the soles of his feet, that is dated 790 A.D. In Buddhist tradition, Buddha's footprint is often used to represent his entire being. This may be another reference to the fact that the entire body is connected to and carried within the soles of the feet. Similarly in India, there exist paintings of the Hindu god Vishnu's feet, with symbols that correspond to several major reflexology points.

MODERN HIS-toe-ry OF REFLEXOLOGY

While the origins of reflexology are ancient, explorations into the scientific basis for reflexology began more recently in Sweden, England, Russia, and Germany. In Sweden around 1834, Per Heinrik Link, the man who introduced Swedish massage to the world, observed that pains originating in certain organs were associated with surfaces on the skin, yet the surface location and the pain seemed wholly unconnected. In the 1890s, Sir Henry Head, a knighted research scientist and medical doctor in England, discovered zones on the skin that became hypersensitive to pressure when an organ connected by nerves to this skin was infected or diseased. He demonstrated the neurological relationship that exists between the skin and the internal organs by mapping areas of reflex zones on the back, which became known as Head Zones.

Around the same time, Russian doctors Ivan Pavlov and Vladimir Bekhterev were exploring reflex respons-es in the body. Pavlov developed the theory of conditioned reflexes. This theory states that there is a simple and direct relationship between a stimulus and a response. He found that almost any stimulus can produce a corresponding conditioned response. So, the Russian perception of reflex therapy evolved from the notion that an afflicted organ is actually receiving the wrong instructions from the brain. The goal of Russian reflex therapy is to interrupt these instructions and even potentially rewrite them!

At the same time in Germany, doctors were also researching the possibilities of treating disease with massage. Dr. Alfons Cornelius observed that pressure to specific areas of the body triggered muscle contractions, changes in blood pressure, variations in warmth and moisture in the body, as well as directly affecting the mental state of the patient. It is believed that in 1893, while Dr. Cornelius recovered from an infection at a spa, he noticed that massage was helpful to the recovery process. In 1902, he published a manuscript called *Pressure Points, The Origin and Significance*, which explained how massage could be applied to "reflex zones" to effectively relieve pain and disease.

While all of this was going on abroad, in 1913, Dr. William Fitzgerald, an American ear, nose, and throat surgeon who had been studying in hospitals in Vienna and London, returned to the United States and introduced reflex therapy to the West. While it still remains a mystery exactly how Dr. Fitzgerald originated his research, the assumption is that he discovered his ideas in Europe and brought them to North America. It is also suggested that in his desire to develop a method of anesthesia and analgesia for minor surgery, Fitzgerald observed that many patients instinctively gripped a chair in response to pain, and so he began to explore that phenomenon in people's hands. Dr. Edwin Bowers, a skeptical medical critic and writer, investigated Dr. Fitzgerald's claims and found the discoveries so exciting that he jointly co-authored a book on this unique therapy.

In a text published in 1917 entitled Zone Therapy, or Relieving Pain at Home, Fitzgerald and Bowers noted that pressure to specific parts of the body could relieve pain and improve the functions of certain organs of the body. For his research, Fitzgerald applied pressure using tight elastic bands to the middle section of each finger, or small clips that he placed on the fingertips. He found that pressure applied to the fingertips could create a local anesthetic effect from the hand, arm, and shoulder, all the way up to the face. Dr. Fitzgerald was actually able to perform minor surgical operations using only this pressure method. In an early experiment, he was even able to demonstrate that a needle could be inserted into a patient's face painlessly, if he applied pressure to the appropriate reflex area on the patient's hand.

In developing this theory, Fitzgerald divided the body into ten equal and vertical zones, ending in the fingers and toes, which correspond to the number of each we have. Fitzgerald found that pressure on one part of a zone could affect everything else within that zone. Therefore, reflex areas on the feet and hands were linked to other areas and organs of the body within the same zone. By exerting pressure on a specific part of the body, Fitzgerald could predict which parts of the body would be affected.

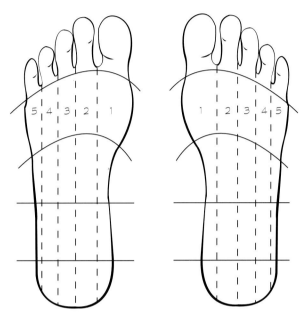

This new theory provoked much interest and cynicism, and Dr. Fitzgerald was under much scrutiny. Nevertheless, his theory on zone therapy was a success, and in an April 29, 1934 newspaper article entitled "Mystery of Zone Therapy Explained," the theory was proven to the world. The article recounts how a famous opera singer approached Dr. Fitzgerald and explained that she was having trouble reaching her high notes. Throat specialists had been unable to diagnose or treat the problem. After examining her fingers and toes, Dr. Fitzgerald traced the problem in her voice to a callus on her right big toe. He applied pressure to the toe for a few moments and the singer observed that she no longer felt pain there. The article stated: "…The doctor asked her to try the tone of the upper register. Miraculously, it would seem to us, the singer reached two tones higher than she had ever done before."

In the 1930s, Dr. Joseph Shelby continued Dr. Fitzgerald's work along with Eunice Ingham, a physiotherapist who worked in Dr. Riley's office. Ingham, who was intrigued with zone therapy, has been credited as the person who further developed and refined zone therapy into what is now known as foot reflexology. In her "trial and error" method, Ingham taped cotton pads over tender areas on her client's feet, and then had her clients walk around while she watched for telltale reactions in the corresponding body part. Ingham studied the connection between areas that she stimulated on the foot and associated problems in the client's organs and glands. She observed that congestion or tension in any part of the foot mirrors congestion or tension in a corresponding part of the body. Thus, when you stimulate the toes there is a related effect in the head, and treating the whole foot can have a relaxing and healing effect on the whole body.

Ingham's theory, which most modern reflexologists still accept as gospel, is that there are energy channels in the body that get blocked by stress and toxins, and when the appropriate area of the foot is manipulated, those channels can be unblocked, allowing the body to regain its natural equilibrium.

Ingham brought her findings to the public and published two books, Stories the Feet Can Tell (1938) and Stories the Feet Have Told (1963). In order to promote and preserve the "Original Ingham Method of Reflex-ology," she later founded The International Institute of Reflexology, which is currently run by her nephew, Dwight C. Byers. (See Suggested Further Reading.) Eunice Ingham practiced and taught reflexology throughout the United States until the age of eighty.

In 1961, physiotherapists objected to the word "therapy" in the name "zone therapy" and consequently, the name "reflexology" was adopted. However, the name "reflexology" was considered illegitimate until another renowned woman in the field of footwork, Mildred Carter, published her book, Helping Yourself with Foot Reflexology, in 1970. When this book was first released, the U.S. Postal Service demanded that the publisher stop all publication of the book because they claimed that the material represented the practice of medicine without a proper license. Fortunately, the publisher's attorneys successfully defended the book and from then on, the name "reflexology" could be used to describe the practice of footwork and reflex therapy. Since then, other names have been adopted for the practices of foot reflexology including pressure point massage, compression massage, pointed pressure massage, and Vita-Flex. In Europe and some other parts of the world, the names zone therapy, reflex zone therapy, and reflexotherapy are still used.

REFLEXOLOGY TODAY

Recently, research studies have been conducted around the world, which validate the effectiveness of reflexology on a wide variety of conditions. As a result, reflexology is quickly being embraced for its provisions of enhancing health, profound relaxation, and pleasure, coupled with its inherent simplicity and harmless nature.

The professional practice of reflexology has been recognized by the national government and integrated into the mainstream provision of health care in four countries: China, Denmark, Japan, and the United Kingdom. In China, where reflexology is accepted by the central government as a means of preventing and curing diseases and preserving health, over three hundred research studies have shown reflexology provided some improvement to ninety-five percent of the over 18,000 cases covering sixty-four illnesses studied. Chronic conditions seem to respond especially well to reflexology. In Denmark, Japan, and the United Kingdom, reflexology has been incorporated into the employee health programs of several large corporations, saving each company thousands of dollars annually in sick leave benefits. As massage therapy (usually seated massage) is slowly being incorporated into many corporations here in the United States, we can only hope that reflexology will soon make its way into offices as an effective employee benefit.

Reflexology is one of the most popular and rapidly growing methods of alternative healing. From nail salons to airport lounges to shopping malls to street fairs, reflexology is offered as a way to ease your aches, pains, and worries away. It's an easy, quick therapy that can affect the entire body, and you don't even have to take your clothes off. And one of the best things is that you can learn to do it to yourself!

PART II:
WESTERN VS. EASTERN HEALING PHILOSOPHY

"Where congestion exists disease will result…
No one can deny the well-known fact that circulation is life; stagnation is death."
Eunice Ingham

CHINESE MEDICINE + ZONE THERAPY = REFLEXOLOGY

Unlike most Western medical therapies, reflexology is a unique, holistic therapy that treats the individual as a whole, integrating the body, mind, and spirit. The theory behind this fascinating science and healing art is a combination of Eastern philosophies and Western scientific research. In essence, East meets West in modern reflexology, which has its roots in both traditional Chinese medicine and zone therapy. To fully understand how reflexology works, it's helpful to familiarize yourself with the elements of both practices and how they work together in the theory of reflexology. In doing so, you can truly appreciate how reflexology blends the science of zone therapy and ancient Chinese holistic heath philosophies into a functional system for wholeness in our daily lives.

In the section that follows, you'll find explanations of the distinctive philosophies of traditional Chinese as well as Western medicine. This will help you understand the cultural differences in the way disease is regarded and treated. In section two, you'll learn about the Eastern and Western scientific theories and the varying concepts of energy in the body. This will give you a foundation to understand reflexology and how it works with your body, or for those to whom you might wish to extend this "touch-ing" gift!

WESTERN HEALING PHILOSOPHY

Disease

For the last century, the predominant mode of healing in our western culture has been disease management. Western medicine tends to approach disease by assuming that it is due to an external force, such as a virus or bacteria, or to a slow degeneration of the functional ability of the body. In traditional Western medicine, which utilizes surgery and pharmaceutical drugs, there is a strong focus on eliminating and alleviating symptoms. This is identified as a "crisis intervention" or "disease management" mode of healing because treatment is focused on specific conditions. When symptoms are identified, a doctor will diagnose the condition and prescribe treatment to manage and eliminate these symptoms. When the symptoms are eliminated or at least managed, the treatment is considered complete.

In Western medicine, there is also a belief that the medical practitioner, rather than the individual, is principally responsible for the body's health. We turn to our doctors for everything from a headache to a backache, and we expect to receive a prescription for some kind of medication to relieve the discomfort. Rather than looking within ourselves and trying to understand the dynamics of what is happening in our lives and how it is affecting our health, we look outside for an answer and a "quick fix" cure. In fact, we often ignore our own body's signals when something hurts or is not functioning properly.

Body, Mind, Spirit

Western medicine is based on the philosophy that the body and mind are separate, in that the body represents one functioning system and the mind another. While this philosophy accepts that each system may affect the other, essentially it sees disease as either physical or mental. Most Western doctors practice with the belief that there is "a pill for every ill," and that an external force, process, or chemical can cure disease. Until only recently, most doctors did not look at a patient's mind to try and understand how it might affect the physical body and even be the cause of disease. As a result, one of the major disadvantages of Western medicine is that it has the potential to cause a great deal of harm, since many diseases can be traced to the mind. In spite of constructive efforts of many who work in the field of mental health, the body and the mind are generally still considered to be separate, and it is the responsibility of the individual to keep the mind under control. As you will see, this is certainly not the case in Eastern ideology. Another significant and striking difference between Western and Eastern philosophy is the lack of awareness and lack of importance placed on the unique significance of touch. In the East, touch is an essential element in medical treatments to subdue pain and fight disease. In fact, in Eastern philosophy the importance of touch has been acknowledged as a primary means to mitigate pain. Here in the West, however, touch is absent from most medical treatments and there has only recently been some advancement in bringing touch, in the form of massage and therapeutic touch, into hospitals and health care facilities.

TRADITIONAL CHINESE HEALING PHILOSOPHY

Disease

One of the major assumptions in traditional Chinese medicine is that disease is due to an internal imbalance of energy. This energy is divided into two basic categories. The first category is female energy, called yin, which represents water, quiet, substance, and night. The second is called yang, and it is male energy. Yang energy represents fire, noise, function, and day. The two energies are polar opposites and their balance determines the state of the body.

Traditional Chinese philosophy believes that treatment of yin/yang energy is an effective means to treat disease. Returning yin and yang to balance restores the body to a healthy state. This highly sophisticated and personal system of health care is a radically different approach to health and disease than Western philosophy because it is "preventative medicine." It focuses on the internal rather than the external of an individual. So much is that the case that for many years, Chinese physicians were not paid until a patient was well and stayed healthy for a certain period of time!

Imbalance = Disease

In Eastern philosophy, when there is an imbalance of energy, the body becomes susceptible to external elements, called pathogens, which can invade the body and cause disease. The essential principle of Chinese traditional medicine is to accurately determine the exact nature of the imbalance between yin and yang, the pathogen causing the trouble, and the means to correct these problems. The patient is treated with energy-balancing therapies, such as acupuncture and shiatsu, which stimulate specific points in order to re-balance the body. As the natural forces return to a normal balance, it improves the body's ability to heal itself, and the condition improves or is cured.

Balance = Health

The Chinese believe that to achieve health and prevent disease it is necessary to maintain a balanced state in the body. In individual terms, the ancient Chinese physicians preached moderation in all things, and they stated that daily activities should include mental as well as physical tasks.

Body, Mind, Spirit

Traditional Chinese medicine's model is holistic. In it, each part of the body is intimately connected, and each organ has a mental as well as a physical function. More specifically, each organ is associated with a particular emotion; for instance, the liver is said to be the organ affected by anger. In this manner, the Chinese do not consider the brain, or subconscious, as separate entities—they interact, and of course, affect each other. This in turn affects the way a disease or imbalance is treated, too.

One great advantage to the Eastern outlook is that it provides a sense of hope. People who suffer from mental problems are made to feel that their disease is real and organic, rather than imagined. Moreover, they are given to believe that real change can indeed happen. For example, instead of being labeled a schizophrenic, the patient understands that the liver is imbalanced and then perceives the disease in a different context. In the West, on the other hand, there is still a stigma attached to depression and other mental illnesses, and individuals who suffer from mental illness may be considered weak because they are unable to "cope." In China, the cultural history and social context of mental disease is different; therefore, people who suffer from mental illness perceive their situations as much more acceptable and natural. In China, there is less "mental disease" as we know it in the West, because a person who would normally be labeled "mentally ill" in the West is often considered to have a disease of the liver or spleen, rather than anxiety or depression, and treated accordingly.

PART III:
ENERGY IN THE BODY

TRADITIONAL CHINESE MERIDIANS

Traditional Chinese methodology is based on the body's channels of vital energy, known as "meridians." These channels carry and distribute energy throughout the body. The best way to understand the flow of energy through the meridians is to compare it to the flow of blood in our veins and arteries. If our blood does not reach our toes, the cells and tissues die and we lose sensitivity. If our blood does not flow freely, we suffer from high or low blood pressure. If our blood clots, we have an embolism or a stroke. Similarly, unbalanced or stagnant energy can cause many diseases and ailments.

When the flow of vital energy through the channels in the body is disrupted, the result is an imbalance that may lead to disease. Every organ of the body is represented by a specific channel of energy, and is categorized as being basically yin or yang. In addition, each meridian is related to one of the five elements (fire, earth, metal, water, and wood). Since the Chinese believe that the five elements comprise the world, they see everything, including all body parts, as falling into a category of one or more elements. What the elements reveal is a connection with specific emotions, spiritual issues, physical characteristics, and temperaments.

Here is a chart of organs that are displayed on the Reflexology Sox™ and their elemental and gender correspondences:

ORGAN	ELEMENT	ENERGY (YIN/YANG)
Heart	Fire	Yin
Small intestine	Fire	Yang
Spleen/Pancreas	Earth	Yin
Stomach	Earth	Yang
Lungs	Metal	Yin
Large intestine	Metal	Yang
Kidneys	Water	Yin
Bladder	Water	Yang
Liver	Wood	Yin
Gall Bladder	Wood	Yang

Along with these designations, there are twelve meridian lines, including six that actually penetrate the major organs and six that are situated in the arms. The six main meridians that penetrate major organs are also (interestingly enough) found in the feet, specifically, the toes. Therefore, stimulating the feet can clear energy blockages and help the body achieve a state of balance! (Hmm, now where have we heard that before?!)

Six Meridians that penetrate
major organs and are found
in the feet:

Six Meridians that do not
penetrate organs:

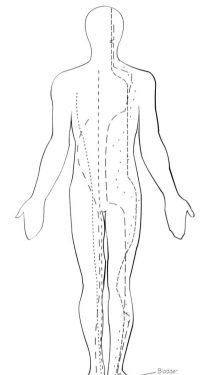

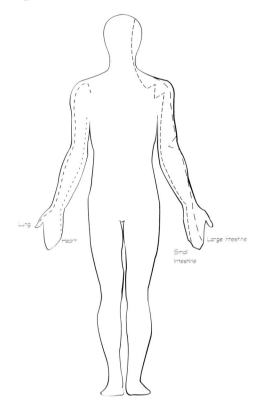

Along these meridians there are over three hundred pressure points, or gateways, where energy can become blocked. These gateways represent points of maximum influence on the flow of vital energy through the channels. Diseases of a particular organ can be identified and treated by stimulating specific pressure points on the channel representing the diseased organ because energy flows; it is not stagnant.

Let's look at this more closely using the example of a torn muscle. The traditional Chinese explanation for this disorder is that the channel of energy running through the damaged muscle has been physically disrupted, and this results in local pain. In order to treat the pain, the flow of vital energy through the channel must be restored. This can be achieved by selecting specific pressure points on the damaged channel and stimulating the points, usually with acupuncture.

Western Zone Therapy and Reflexology

In the West, the concept of how energy flows through the body is based on the work of Dr. William Fitzgerald, who developed the "zone therapy" theory in the early 1900s, and Eunice Ingham, whose work on zone therapy became the contemporary basis for reflexology (See earlier this chapter). Zone therapy states that rather than meridians, there are ten zones throughout the body. Five of these zones are located on the right side of the body and five are on the left; one corresponds to each toe or finger. These zones can be compared to the wiring in a house in that the reflexes travel through the zones in a similar way to electricity traveling through wires. Therefore, zones are used in determining various locations of reflexes within the feet and hands.

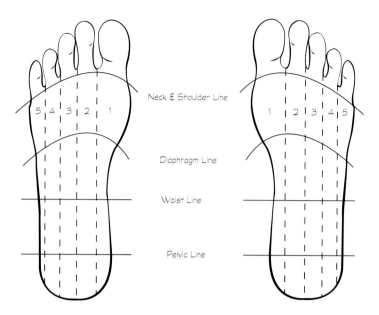

As in Eastern ideology, zone therapy is based on the idea that stress and toxins can block zones. Congestion or tension in any part of the foot mirrors congestion or tension in a corresponding part of the body. Therefore, when the appropriate area of the foot is manipulated, those congested channels can be unblocked, which allows the body to regain its natural equilibrium.

The feet are a mirror of the body in that each foot is divided into areas and zones. In reflexology, each foot represents half of the body, the left foot corresponding to the left side and the right foot corresponding to the right side. A reflex area for every part of your body is located on the sole of each foot in a map that resembles the map of the human body. To locate specific reflex areas, it's useful to understand the four lines that divide the foot and the body. Each foot is divided horizontally and vertically into five areas, which correspond to certain areas of the body.

The four horizontal lines that divide the foot are:

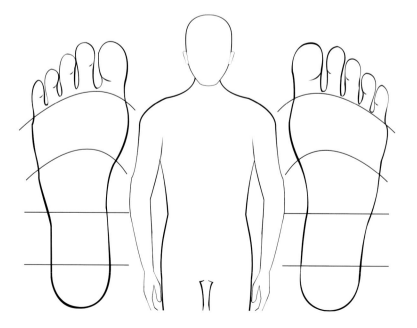

Each foot is also divided into five vertical zones, running from the toes to the heel, which correspond to five zones of the body. You can locate specific reflex points on the foot by studying these divisions and zones and understanding the areas of the body to which they correspond.

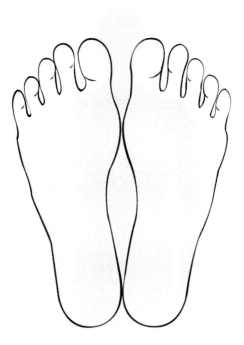

Understanding Reflexology

Although Eastern and Western medical philosophies of how to heal the body and keep it healthy are radically different, reflexology is unique because it successfully integrates both philosophies into its theory and technique. In spite of their diverse philosophical assumptions, reflexology regards these two medical systems as mutually beneficial, rather than mutually exclusive. Given that each system has ideas and therapeutic methods that can be explained both scientifically and philosophically, they can both benefit the individual. In reflexology, East meets West in a cooperative spirit that can broaden the philosophical, methodological, and ideological basis of medicine, and in turn, aid our quest for mental, spiritual, and physical wholeness.

Chapter 2:
Baring Your Sole

"THERE'S LANGUAGE IN HER EYE, HER CHEEKS, HER LIPS.
NAY, HER FOOT SPEAKS."

Shakespeare, *Troilus and Cressida*

PART I:
WHAT IS REFLEXOLOGY?

Reflexology is an ancient healing art and a holistic healing technique that aims to treat the body, mind, and spirit. The term holisitic is derived from the word *holos*, which means whole. Reflexology is an integrative health science that does not isolate a disease and treat its symptoms, but rather supports the whole person by nurturing a state of balance and harmony. It tries to get to the root of the disease. This gentle therapy encourages the body to heal itself at its own pace, often counteracting a lifetime of misuse.

The art of reflexology is not the same as a foot massage or massage therapy. Rather than simply rubbing randomly, reflexology treats the feet as a microcosm of the entire body. It is based on the theory that there are zones and reflex areas in the feet and hands, which correspond to all glands, organs, and systems of the body. By applying pressure using thumb, finger, and hand techniques to these reflex areas, you can relax and rejuvenate every part of the body, reduce stress, and promote physiological changes to improve your overall well-being. Reflexology can naturally conquer many health problems, and also serves as a form of preventative maintenance. It's a safe, easy, and beneficial method of treatment that can help you take responsibility for and become more intimately involved with your own health. What's more, it heightens your own body awareness.

The human body is highly intelligent and has a remarkable, built-in, self-correcting system that can restore health to diseased areas. The goal of reflexology, in effect, is to re-educate, re-pattern, and re-condition nerves so that the body can heal itself by using that self-correcting system. Better still, reflexology is a safe, non-invasive, complementary health practice that facilitates on-going physical, emotional, and spiritual improvements.

REFLEXOLOGY VS. MASSAGE

Many people confuse reflexology with massage, and mistakenly refer to reflexology as a "foot massage." To set the record straight, reflexology is not massage, nor is it a medical treatment. Rather, it is a fascinating holistic healing technique that works with the energy flow of the body to promote natural self-healing. Reflexology is based on the theory that when the body's energy pathways become blocked, the body experiences various levels of discomfort. Reflexology's goal is to assist in reviving one's energy flow and bring the body back into homeostasis, a state of balance. While both reflexology and massage share the same goal, which is to enhance the well-being of the client, they are two different modalities with their own individual strengths. Reflexology has its own history, vocabulary, theories, and techniques that are separate from any other profession. Although both involve the use of the hands to apply their techniques, there are several important differences between the two disciplines:

1. Massage is the systematic manipulation of soft tissues of the body, while reflexology is the application of specific pressure to reflex points in the hands and feet. The effect of reflexology is seen at a distance from where the pressure is applied; its intent is not to change the soft tissue of the body.

2. Massage works through the musculature, while reflexology works through the nervous system.

3. Massage employs many different types of strokes to directly affect specific areas of the body, while reflexology uses on and off pressure with the thumbs and fingers to indirectly stimulate many areas that an individual might not otherwise be able to affect.

WHAT CAN REFLEXOLOGY DO FOR ME?

Incorporating reflexology into an overall healthy lifestyle can be quite beneficial. The reflex areas in the feet and hands correspond to all the parts of the body, including internal organs, therefore this treatment offers a "hands-on" way to heal the whole body and maintain that health. Reflexology has been found to be beneficial for a wide range of disorders, including headaches, sinus congestion, stiffness in the back and neck, digestion, and hormonal problems. Additionally, reflexology can bring you soothing stress relief and relax not only your feet, but your entire body as well. It can improve circulation, ease pain, and boost energy. Most people who try reflexology find they benefit from it to some degree; the problem either clears up completely or the symptoms decrease. The treatment can be extremely relaxing and pleasurable to receive, as well as stimulating and invigorating.

TOP TEN BENEFITS OF REFLEXOLOGY

1. Stress Relief

Whether you suffer from insomnia, chronic fatigue, stomach problems, or migraines, the root of many common health problems can be linked to stress. Stress can be caused by mental, emotional, physical, or environmental factors, and in this hi-tech, fast-paced society, it's almost impossible to avoid it completely. Stress can be quite damaging to the body and mind. It's well known that an individual trying to function while under the influence of prolonged stress is less capable of defending against illnesses and repairing damage caused by injury.

Since reflexology is primarily a relaxation technique, it can counteract the effects of stress as it helps the body relax. Through the relaxation process, the body is more capable of dealing with the stresses placed on it by daily living and strains associated with illness. Reflexology gently nudges the body toward better functioning by relaxing the muscles, encouraging better circulation, and improving the functions of all body systems to promote better overall outlooks (when you feel good, it's much easier to be positive).

It's safe to say that stress, which can make us age more quickly and become physically ill and emotionally upset, is the enemy. Reflexology, on the other hand, can become a friend you have right at your fingertips!

2. Muscle Relaxation

Many factors besides stress can cause your muscles to tighten up. Too much time spent sitting in one position, holding a phone or heavy bag on the same side, working out with weights, being a "weekend warrior," and emotional problems are but a few common causes. Whatever the source may be, when your muscles are tense and overstressed, the energy in your body is thrown off balance. Specifically, the energy in the nerve pathway that connects those muscles with the rest of your body becomes congested. This can lead to fatigue, pain, irritability, and worst of all, more stress.

By stimulating the reflex areas to the parts of the body that are stressed, reflexology can help unblock the energy in the nerves and relax your muscles. Consider for a moment: There are over 7,000 nerves in your feet! By touching these nerves (i.e. rubbing the whole foot) you can affect the reflex areas in the entire body. This then restores physical harmony and relieves a lot of unwanted and unhealthy muscle tension.

3. Circulation Improvement

In order for all of the body's systems to function properly, it's essential for blood to circulate and reach every cell. The blood carries nutrients and oxygen to the tissues and if, for some reason, the blood can't reach a specific area, the cells in that area will starve and die. When you are stressed, your breathing often becomes shallow and the circulation of blood becomes sluggish. As a result, the tissues can become oxygen-deprived, the energy in your body depleted and unstable, and all of your body systems suffer.

To keep your body's circulation running smoothly, reflexology helps by encouraging steady blood flow to and from the heart. This improves the flow of oxygenated blood to all of your cells, which then rejuvenates tired tissues and delivers proper nutrition to them.

4. Detoxify and Cleanse

Getting rid of waste and toxins is extremely important to your health. The human body has built-in systems to process and eliminate what it does not need, and it's necessary for good health that these systems remain unblocked. When the lymphatic, urinary, or intestinal systems are blocked due to a buildup of toxins and waste, the energy in the body stagnates. You may feel lethargic, bloated, and even sick. When you "can't go" it's a terrible feeling. To maintain a healthy, unblocked body you must get rid of the garbage that can damage your system. Reflexology can encourage your body to "let go" and eliminate toxins and waste that upset your body and your mood!

5. Body Systems Balancer

Balance is vital to being healthy in body, mind, and spirit. For the body to keep running smoothly, it strives to maintain a state of homeostasis, which is equilibrium among the various functions and chemical compositions of fluids and tissues. A balance of energy in the body is also crucial to good health. When there is a malfunction in some area of the body, it is natural for the balance in that area to be thrown off. Every part of the body is interconnected, so when there is an imbalance in one area, it almost always leads to an imbalance in another. It's sort of like a complex, foreign car; when one thing goes wrong, it starts the domino effect and one thing after another goes wrong. To fix the car, you must start from the beginning and repair the damage from the first problem outward. That's reflexology's goal—to promote and sustain balance in every organ, gland, muscle, tissue, and system of the body starting from the source of a problem and moving outward. By relaxing the muscles and sending healing energy throughout the body, reflexology can reestablish and stabilize a healthy equilibrium.

6. Vitality Renewal

Do you have enough energy? Most people don't. Individuals who suffer from low levels of energy may find that everything is exhausting and most things, including people, seem to suck what little energy you do have right out of you. Like a battery that needs to be recharged, your body, mind, and spirit also need recharging occasionally.

Energy flows through the universe and it is always available when you need it. You have seven primary energy centers, or chakras, in your body, and at any given moment any one of them may be suffering from a lack of energy or an imbalance in energy flow. Reflexology can help by sending new energy through the chakras to the whole body, rejuvenating and invigorating every cell of your being. This new vitality can open congested energy pathways, stimulate your spirit, and bring a new level of consciousness to your life.

7. Pain Relief

Whenever you feel pain anywhere in your body, your brain is sending you a signal that something is wrong. Normally, when medication is used to relieve pain, the pain may disappear but the problem is still there. This can do even more harm to the body because the warning signals from the brain are blocked. For example, if you take a painkiller to relieve the pain from a sprained ankle, you will continue to walk as usual without feeling the twinges of pain that are your body's way of saying, "Don't put any weight on this ankle." Consequently, you may do more damage because you cannot "hear" this natural warning.

Reflexology is a natural painkiller. By focusing on specific reflex areas, unblocking the pathways where energy may be stuck, and balancing the energy in the rest of the body, reflexology can effectively relieve pain and send healing energy to rest of the body. However, don't ignore your aches and pains. Use reflexology as a temporary helper and then get busy finding out what's causing the problem!

8. Early Problem Detection

Have you ever heard the expression, "If it ain't broke, don't fix it"? Reflexology is preventative health care that aims to strengthen the body so that it doesn't get to the point where you have to "fix" it. By understanding the reflex areas of the feet and their connection to corresponding body parts, you can determine when something in the body is out of balance and may be malfunctioning (often by detecting a grainy area in the reflex point). Employing reflexology for those detected problem areas clears energy blockages that may contribute to the problem, and may also prevent future blockages.

9. Nurtures Loving Relationships

Touch is a very powerful element in human bonding. For babies, it's essential to their survival. Unfortunately, it's often lacking in today's high-tech, fast-paced world. Reflexology can bring the power of touch into daily life, and help couples spend intimate, relaxing, and therapeutic time together.

When you touch someone with your hands and your heart, you exchange energy and communicate love and compassion. You don't have to be a massage therapist to be able to bring relaxation and stress relief to someone else. Even a five-minute foot treatment can convey how much you care and can strengthen your relationship. What's more, reflexology offers a technique that stimulates the sex organs and can heat things up in the bedroom. Why not give it a try?

10. Integrates Body, Mind, and Spirit

Traditionally, Western medicine is based on the philosophy that the body represents one functioning system, and the mind represents another. It accepts that each system may affect the other, but essentially it sees disease as either physical or mental. Chinese medicine, on the other hand, regards the body as a whole. It considers each part of the human design as intimately connected, and each organ as having a mental as well as a physical function. Disease is perceived as an imbalance in the energy lines within the body. It occurs when you're not "at ease."

Reflexology reflects the theory of Chinese medicine in that it sees the body, mind, and spirit as a cooperative whole, and treats the body in its entirety. By opening and balancing energy in the nerve pathways, reflexology not only relieves physical problems, but it clears out emotional debris as well. Reflexology also helps us learn to balance the energy of the body, mind, and soul. It is a valuable means to integrate these three essential aspects of humankind.

WHAT'S SO UNIQUE ABOUT OUR FEET?

7,000 Nerve Endings
26 Bones
107 Ligaments
19 Muscles

Did you know that over a lifetime the average person walks approximately 100,000 miles, which is the equivalent of four times around the earth, yet many people pay closer attention to their car's tires than to their own feet? The human foot has over 7,000 nerve endings, twenty-six bones, 107 ligaments, and nineteen muscles. Sadly, most people neglect this significant part of the body, which provides a foundation for the rest of the body, until something happens and they feel discomfort or pain.

Many years ago, when humans existed in a "barefoot society," the soles of the feet were stimulated by every step that was taken. Essentially, walking barefoot on the earth was and still is a natural reflexology treatment. When humans started wearing shoes, however, we lost that direct contact with the earth and were no longer grounded to it. In trying to protect the soles of our feet, we lost the natural exchange between the body's electrical current and the energy of the earth. Reflexology can reawaken the feet and recharge the energy flow that used to come from walking barefoot.

As stress, illness, or inactivity cause the muscle tissue in our feet to weaken, our bloodstream becomes congested. Without the full cleansing power of the blood supply, waste matter collects in the feet, forming crystal-like deposits. The feet are "worked" to break down these deposits that build up around the reflexes and nerve endings to improve circulation, increase energy, and help the body get back on a positive health track.

Recently, much attention and research has been dedicated to the feet because they represent a unique image of the body. Basically, the feet are a microsystem that reflects every part of the body. Supposedly, there are at least fifteen microsystems in the human body, including the hands and ears, which have similar reflex areas to the feet. An easy way to understand this is to imagine a shrunken image of yourself superimposed on the soles of your feet, with the right side or your body on the right foot, and the left side of the body on the left foot. Every part of your body falls in to place on the sole of each foot, like a map. This is also true of the other microsystems:

Hands:

Hand reflexology uses the same techniques as foot reflexology. Until recently, it was believed that the reflex-es in the hands were not as easily stimulated as those in the feet. However, this outlook has changed. Most reflexologists now believe that working on the hands can be just as effective as working on the feet and, consequently, interest in hand reflexology is increasing. Since there has been less work with the hands in the past, the locations of the reflexes in the hands are not as well established.

Ears:

Ear reflexology evolved from acupuncture of the ears. The ear is an extremely complex, yet easily accessible, sensory organ that has hundreds of pressure points. For centuries, acupuncturists have used needles to stimulate reflex areas in the ears in order to promote health in the rest of the body. (You're probably thinking, "Ouch!" Actually, it doesn't hurt at all.) Ear reflexology, on the other hand, consists of physical stimulation of the reflex areas of the ears without the use of needles. It does employ finger-pressure techniques, but slightly different ones than those applied to the feet and hands.

Returning to the "sole" issue—the feet often take a severe beating as we cram them into shoes that are too tight and proceed to walk for miles, creating self-induced foot problems for the sake of "a pretty shoe." One of the most important reasons to work on the feet is to give them some relief from the torture they habitually endure and provide a positive support system for the entire body. Additionally, there are several more reasons why you should use foot reflexology:

1. The feet are the least vulnerable part of the body.

The feet are the farthest body part from the head, which is naturally the most vulnerable part of the body. Therefore, those who are uncomfortable with conventional massage may find this technique less threatening and more "user friendly." We see a particularly positive response in babies who cannot always accept other forms of stimulation.

2. Poor circulation.

Since the feet are the farthest body part from the head, they are susceptible to poor circulation. People who suffer from poor circulation may have cold, tender, or swollen hands and feet.

Stimulating them with reflexology can improve circulation and encourage the flow of blood to the extremities.

3. Toxin buildup.

As we walk around, gravity pushes the toxins in our body down to our feet. The effects of gravity, combined with poor circulation, can lead to the build-up of inorganic waste materials, such as uric acid and calcium crystals, in the soles of the feet. These toxins form "grainy" areas in our feet that are often tender to the touch. These areas aren't hard to find, since they have a very different feel from the rest of the foot. Besides being a sign of waste build-up, they serve a purpose in that they frequently indicate a problem with the corresponding organ.

WHO CAN BENEFIT FROM REFLEXOLOGY?

Reflexology is a safe, natural healing technique that can benefit everyone from a newborn baby girl to an eighty-year-old man. It can even benefit pets! This gentle art can bring relief from a wide range of acute and chronic conditions. But since no two people are the same, the benefits that reflexology brings will be different for everyone. However, everybody can reap the natural benefits that come with relaxation and the rebalancing of energy.

Reflexology seems to be most beneficial for people suffering from stress-related disorders, such as lower back pain, chronic indigestion, headaches, and high blood pressure. It is also quite useful in treating emotional problems, such as depression, sexual dysfunction, and eating disorders. Today, an increasing number of people are using this natural therapy as a way of simply relaxing, balancing, and harmonizing the body.

CAN ANYONE DO REFLEXOLOGY?

Reflexology is simple, and everyone can do it. No expensive equipment is required, and you do not need to be a massage therapist or take a reflexology class to learn to give an effective treatment. Just relax and let your hands move freely. Let intuition be your guide as you feel the foot for tenderness and areas that are "grainy". As you get more comfortable touching your feet (or someone else's), you'll be able to tell where the body is out of balance and in need of extra attention. With Reflexology Sox™, it's easy to figure out where the reflex points for specific parts of the body are located. Just put them on and you're on your way to a fabulous reflexology treatment.

If you're interested in becoming a reflexologist, there is information on schools and certification at the end of the book. Currently, there is no national licensure for reflexology, therefore the background and training of reflexologists will vary. There is a voluntary national certification program, as well as several well-established institutes, such as the International Institute of Reflexology, that offer reflexologist referrals.

DO I NEED A PARTNER OR CAN I DO IT MYSELF?

One of the best things about reflexology is that it does not require two people. In fact, many people find self-reflexology more effective because only you know exactly what you are feeling as your fingers touch your feet. You, better than anyone, can gauge how deep the finger pressure should be, and you'll know exactly when you've gone too deep. Reflexology is a great way for you to get to know your own body.

If you have a partner, you can practice the techniques on each other and get comfortable touching someone else's feet. As you work on each other, it's important to communicate about how different finger pressures feel and any sensitivity that occurs. Even if you plan on using reflexology regularly with a partner, I highly recommend practicing on your own feet so that you get to know how your hands might feel on someone else.

Is reflexology ever not recommended?

Since reflexology treats the whole person, not just the symptoms of the disease, it can help everyone stay balanced and strong. While historically, reflexology has been found to have a positive effect on the body suffering from a wide variety of chronic problems, it is not a solution for all ills. Though reflexology can do no harm, there are three conditions of which you should remain aware and cautious:

1. Thrombosis, the formation of a blood clot in a blood vessel, is a condition that might be aggravated by reflexology, since stimulation might move the clot.

2. Diabetes is a condition that often requires insulin to balance blood sugar levels. Since reflexology can stimulate the pancreas to produce insulin, it may affect the body's insulin level and change the effect of the prescribed amount.

3. Pregnancy. Avoid reflexology during the first three months of pregnancy and use caution while pregnant, as labor can be induced by direct and strong stimulation of the reflex areas to the reproductive organs.

In addition, reflexology is not recommended in the case of serious systemic diseases, where increased circulation might cause the infection to spread, and also in the case of injuries to the feet. If you have any specific concerns about the safety of reflexology, consult your physician. Reflexology can be used as a complement to any type of medical approach or therapy, but it is not intended as a substitute for medical treatment.

PART II:
WHAT TO EXPECT FROM A REFLEXOLOGY TREATMENT

If you've never had a reflexology treatment before, you probably have many questions. Before you give or get a reflexology treatment, it's important to understand how reflexology works and what you can expect from a session. To this end, the following questions and answers should tell you everything you want or need to know.

What will I feel during the treatment?

Reflexology consists of special techniques that are designed to stimulate all of the reflex areas of the feet to bring about profound relaxation. Most people feel a peaceful serenity come over them as the feet are stimulated, and some even fall asleep. Sometimes you may feel the pressure applied to the foot and be aware of a slight discomfort or tenderness. This is normal and is only a sign that there is congestion in that area. Tender spots indicate areas that need extra attention. As you get (or give yourself) regular treatments, these sensitive areas will become less tender.

Reflexology should not hurt. In other words, "pain is not gain" in a reflexology treatment. Pressure, as in regular massage, should be strong, but not uncomfortable. The degree of discomfort that you may feel is indicative of the differing imbalances in the body. Remarkably, reflexology will relax you while stimulating your body's own healing mechanisms.

How long does a reflexology session last?

Normally, a professional reflexology session lasts thirty to sixty minutes. However, since the benefits of reflexology can be obtained in just a few minutes, shorter sessions are also extremely effective. If you've ever received a foot massage, you know how great it feels, especially in the first moment that a person's hands touch the soles of your feet. You feel like you're melting and every part of your body just relaxes. Imagine thirty minutes of this. It's pure bliss. Even if you're working on your own feet, with every minute you're erasing the effects of stress, and rubbing away tensions in your body and mind.

How fast are the results?

It's not uncommon to get results from just one reflexology treatment. I have worked on clients who complain of intense sinus pressure. After several minutes of stimulating their toes, which is the reflex area to the sinuses, they can feel their sinuses begin to clear up and the pressure and pain subside. Other clients have come to me complaining of unbearable lower back pain; at the end of the treatment, during which I've stimulated the reflex areas to the lower back, they stand up and are amazed at the difference they feel. Whether they feel an immediate change in their bodies or not, everybody I have ever worked on says they feel relaxed and rejuvenated at the end of a treatment. Even the five-minute quickie treatments!

Sometimes, the effects of reflexology happen gradually. Every body is different, and some are more receptive to reflexology than others. For chronic illnesses, such as asthma or arthritis, I find that it takes several regular treatments to effect a change in the body. However, be aware that while you may not notice a difference right away, even just one treatment activates the body's natural healing abilities. Herring's Law, which is a universally-accepted guideline for healing through homeopathic therapies, states that for a chronic condition to improve, you should allow at least three months plus at least one more month for every year the person has had the condition. The number of treatments per month varies by the condition and the severity of the symptoms. For chronic conditions, I recommend using reflexology daily on yourself and seeing a professional reflexologist once or twice a month.

How long do the results last?

Since the intention and goal of reflexology is to unblock areas of congestion and balance the energy in your body, the results from a reflexology treatment will last as long as the energy remains free flowing and undisturbed. Since everybody is different, and no two individuals' environments and stress tolerance levels are the same, the results vary. Sometimes, the peace and overall well-being that you feel after a reflexology treatment will last a week or longer.

Other times, even if you have almost the same exact treatment, the results will only last a day. To extend the length of the results, I recommend using reflexology on yourself daily, even for just a few minutes. This way, you may be able to achieve a state of balanced energy that remains consistent and stable for much longer periods of time.

WHEN DO I NEED A REFLEXOLOGY TREATMENT?

Getting a reflexology treatment is a little bit like getting a massage. Some people will do it when they have a specific health concern and they want the therapeutic benefit. Others will turn to reflexology when they have a particularly high level of stress and tension in their lives (and in their bodies). Other people still, who fall in love with having their feet rubbed and the benefits that follow, include regular sessions of reflexology as part of their health regimen and a preventative approach to health care. Finally, there are those people who indulge themselves in reflexology treatments regularly simply for the positive sensations and the profound relaxation that they enjoy.

HOW OFTEN SHOULD I USE REFLEXOLOGY?

If you have the time—and all it really takes is five minutes—I believe you can and should use reflexology every day. If you have a partner, reflexology is a great way to relax and reconnect. It's also a wonderful way to bring touch into your life on a daily basis. Not only will you reap the benefits of stress relief, rebalanced energy, and improved circulation, you will activate the body's natural healing abilities to strengthen your immune system and prevent disease.

HOW MANY TREATMENTS DO I NEED?

For chronic conditions, I recommend having one session per week. For optimum general health and preventative measures, once a month is sufficient. For the periods in between your treatments, I suggest you practice the same techniques on your own feet or perhaps have a partner help you with "mini-treatments" during the rest of the week.

WHAT CAN I EXPECT AFTER MY FIRST TREATMENT?

After the first reflexology treatment, most people feel relaxed and invigorated. A few hours after treatment, it's normal that some internal cleansing will take place. Therefore, it is recommended that you drink plenty of water. You may also want to take a hot bath to help your body process. Since reflexology opens up energy pathways that were previously congested or closed, your body may respond in a very definite way. You may have a feeling of well-being and relaxation or you may feel lethargic, nauseous, or tearful, but this is just transitory.

It's normal to feel more emotional, open, and even vulnerable. This is a sign that you are adjusting to the new flow of energy. Take this opportunity to "go within" and listen to your inner voice. Take care of yourself and be sensitive to whatever feelings may arise. This is an opportunity for you to become aware of the subtle energy shifts that are taking place in your body.

The body remembers many things that we do not, and it holds physical and emotional memories in different areas. Sometimes, reflexology can stimulate areas of the body that may bring up sensitive, emotional issues. When this happens, you may feel overcome by unexpected feelings from the past. Experiencing these feelings, then allowing your body to "process" and let them go, can help release the memories from your body. By affecting your emotions, reflexology becomes much more than an effective physical therapy; it can help integrate and heal your body, mind, and soul.

What do I need to give a reflexology treatment?

Other than your hands, all you need is a calm environment and a comfortable place to sit. If you have the Reflexology Sox™, put them on your feet or your partner's, and stimulate the entire foot, focusing on the reflex areas that may be in need of extra attention. Or, you can work on the naked foot, using the different horizontal body lines and vertical zones to locate specific reflex areas. Even if you can't determine the location of particular reflex areas, simply stimulating the soles of the feet will affect the entire body. You may want to use a little bit of lotion or massage oil to spread over the feet, but use very little (maybe a teaspoon at the most) so your fingers can glide over the feet but don't become too slippery. If you accidentally use too much, have a towel handy to wipe off any excess.

If you are using a reflexology chart to locate specific reflex areas, you should be aware that not all charts are the same. Just as every body is different, the maps to the soles of the feet are also different. However, this does not mean that they are wrong. Most reflexology charts will give you a good idea of approximately where you will find a specific reflex area. It's your job to look at each foot individually, locate the horizontal body lines and vertical zones, and then feel the foot to determine where the corresponding body parts are situated. Take your time with this and learn from the process. The more you become aware of uniqueness in your own feet or those of your partner, the more effective reflexology will become.

Part III:
Preparing for a Reflexology Treatment

Now that you understand what reflexology is, it's time to get started on your first treatment. If you're worried about giving someone, or yourself, a treatment for the first time, relax and take a deep breath. You can't do anything wrong and no one can get hurt. Here's a thought to keep in the back of your mind: Even if you do nothing else but hold the feet in your hands, you will produce a relaxing and calming effect that can balance and renew energy in the entire body. The reflexology techniques offered in this book can be used as guidelines in your practice, or you can create techniques on your own. Let your hands be your guide and don't worry about what you think a treatment should be. Open up to the intuitive part of yourself, and have fun!

People are always amazed by the simplicity and baffled by the results of reflexology. When it comes to pain relief and good health, I suggest you "let your fingers do the walking" by practicing reflexology on yourself. Here are some suggestions for things you can do to make your reflexology treatments the best they can be. You don't have to do all or any of them. Obviously, if you only have five minutes, the only thing you can do is sit down, take your shoes off, and start working those feet! For a great reflexology treatment, just do whatever makes you or your partner comfortable and relaxed.

TAKE A SOLE SOAK

Before beginning a reflexology treatment on yourself or someone else, a nice hot soak in a foot-bath or bathtub can help you loosen up and get your mind off of the day's worries. A relaxing foot-soak can also help get rid of any stinky foot odor, a very common problem after a long day during which feet are perspiring in tight socks and shoes. There are over 250,000 sweat glands in your feet and when you cram them into a warm, dark, closed space for several hours, you end up with hot, sweaty feet. When this happens, the bacteria on the skin multiply and your feet start to smell. To prevent stinky feet, the best thing to do is keep them from perspiring. To get rid of foot odor, add six tablespoons of Epson salts to a quart of warm water and soak.

To enhance your bath with aromatherapy (and further eliminate foot odor), you can add a few drops of essential oil. (See Aromatherapy section, page 42.) If you don't want to take a bath, try sitting on the side of tub and let your feet just dangle in a few inches of warm water. Flex your feet, point and flex your toes… Loosen up. The hot water not only soothes and cleans your feet, but it also prepares them for further stimulation. Water symbolizes cleansing and "new life" in many religions, and I believe that by soaking your feet in water you cleanse them of negative energy, and prepare them to absorb new, positive, healing energy. After a hot foot-bath, I feel like my feet are more sensitive to the touch and are, of course, squeaky clean.

GETTING COMFORTABLE

Choose a room that is warm, quiet, and peaceful. You may want to play some relaxing music, dim the lights, and use candles. Burning incense or using aromatherapy oils can help open your senses and create a sensual mood. Do whatever you need to do to stop the "chatter" in your mind. If you're planning to give yourself the reflexology treatment, you may be most comfort-able in a chair or on a sofa, with pillows behind your back for support. Cross one foot over your knee, and turn the sole of your foot upward, so you can see it. Pull your foot in towards you to reach the sole more comfortably. If this is uncomfortable, try sitting "Indian-style" and see if you can grab hold of the top foot. Go with whichever way works for you without feeling like a pretzel (if you're terribly uncomfortable, the effects achieved from reflexology decrease).

If you're working on someone else, there are several positions you can use:

1. Partners: If you and your partner want to give each other reflexology treatments at the same time, I suggest sitting face to face on opposite ends of a couch. This way, you can both take one of your partner's feet in your hands and work on them at the same time. By facing each other, you can easily communicate how your partner's hands feel and if she hits a tender area. In the beginning, it's important to give your partner feedback—whether good or bad—so that she can learn what areas are sensi-tive and how her touch feels to you. The more you communicate, the better the treatment will be. Place a pillow under both of your knees for extra support.

2. Treatment on the couch: The same position that partners use to give each other simultaneous treatments can also be used if only one person is giving the treatment.

3. Treatment from a chair: Some people find it more comfortable to give treatments while sitting in a chair. If your partner is sitting on a couch or chair, or lying back on

a massage table or bed, place your chair about one foot from the edge so you can comfortably take one foot in your hands without having to reach too far.

4. On the floor: If you prefer to sit on the floor, have your partner either lean back against a wall or a couch, or lie down on her back. Place your partner's feet on top of a firm pillow in front of you. Depending on your arm length, you may want to place the pillow in your lap for ease of access and movement. Make sure that your arms aren't reaching or bent too much. Remember, it's as important for you to be comfortable as it is for your partner to be relaxed.

REFLEXOLOGY SOX™ VS. BARE FEET

If you have the Reflexology Sox™, I suggest that you put them on and use them to help you learn the location of the important reflex areas. The Sox™ are made of a smooth nylon/lycra microfiber so they actually allow you to feel what's going on underneath the skin. The design on the bottom will be your guide to direct you to the important reflex areas that may need stimulation. Later, as you get to know where the reflex areas to specific parts of the body are located on each foot, you can take the Sox™ off and try working directly on bare feet. When you touch the skin directly, you can better feel changes in the skin, as well as those "grainy" areas that indicate that there may be something wrong with the corresponding part of the body.

If you don't have the Reflexology Sox™ (maybe you lost them or gave them away to some lucky individual!), I suggest that you work on bare feet. Socks, especially thick athletic or woolen socks, may interfere with your ability to really feel the foot and what is going on under the skin. One of the benefits of reflexology is the ability to discover areas of the body that may have some sort of congestion in their energy pathway, and then to open the blocked pathway before it becomes damaging to the body. It's difficult to do this with socks on because it can send mixed sensual cues to your hands, not all of which are accurate. In addition, you can see the natural lines on a bare foot, and you'll be better able to locate specific reflex areas using those unique lines. If you're concerned about hygiene, I recommend getting some antibacterial lotion, gel, or spray to use on funky feet.

LOTION VS. OIL VS. NOTHING

If you are using the Reflexology Sox™, you will not need any lotion or oil. The Sox™ are smooth and will allow your fingers to glide easily on the feet. If you're working on bare feet, you may want to use a small amount of oil or lotion to help your fingers slide over the skin more evenly. If you're using lotion, use about a teaspoon at a time. You may have to reapply a few times for each foot, but it's better than having so much that you can't see the lines on the foot. Too much oil will lead to a slick and your hands will slither all over the place. You might want to use aromatherapy oils that are suited to healing or relaxation, like lavender or tea tree, for this purpose. (See Aromatherapy chart in the following section.) In either case, it's best to have a towel handy for accidental lotion or oil slip-ups.

Many reflexologists prefer to work with no lotion or oil, just bare feet, or sometimes skin combined with a little talcum powder. This prevents fingers from slipping so that you can apply pressure to specific reflex points. I personally prefer using a little lotion, usually scented with peppermint or eucalyptus, which I find invigorating and refreshing. I don't like to use oil because the feet tend to get too slippery and then, after the treatment, clients walk away with "greasy" feet.

AROMATHERAPY FOR REFLEXOLOGY

Aromatherapy is an easy way to enhance your reflexology treatment. Aromatherapy is the art of using pure essential oils derived from nature to enhance overall well-being. Just a few drops of an essential oil added to lotion or good quality massage oil (such as almond, grape-seed, peanut, or wheat-germ oils) can nourish the skin, enrich the senses, and soothe the soul. Different oils evoke different feelings and moods, and can create a certain "vibe" for your treatment. I generally like to use the more stimulating oils, such as eucalyptus, peppermint, and juniper, to really "wake up" the feet and the mind. In addition, I always add a few drops of tea tree oil, which has a natural anti-viral agent, and lavender, which has natural antibacterial properties. As you experiment with different oil combinations, you'll find which oils work best for you.

The chart below describes some of the effects of several aromatic essential oils that work well with reflexology.

OIL	AROMA	EMOTIONAL EFFECT
Bergamot	Fresh, citrus, lively	Uplifting, encouraging
Cedarwood	Warm, woody, soft	Calming, comforting
Chamomile	Light, floral	Soothing, relaxing
Eucalyptus	Refreshing, clean, penetrating	Stimulating, cleansing
Frankincense	Spicy, woody	Calming, strengthening
Geranium	Sweet, floral, clean	Calming, balancing
Juniper	Fruity, refreshing	Uplifting, detoxifying
Lavender	Fresh, floral, clean	Soothing, relaxing, balancing
Lemon	Citrus, clean, fresh	Stimulating, refreshing
Lemongrass	Sweet, grassy	Refreshing, rejuvenating
Orange	Citrus, lively, fresh	Cheering, relaxing
Peppermint	Strong, minty	Invigorating, stimulating
Rosemary	Clean, strong	Uplifting, rejuvenating
Sandalwood	Warm, woody	Relaxing, sensual
Tea Tree	Strong, fresh	Cleansing, stimulating
Thyme	Herbal, intense	Stimulating, strengthening
Vetiver	Earthy, woody	Comforting, balancing
Ylang-Ylang	Sweet, flowery	Sensual, arousing

How to begin

I always begin a reflexology treatment by first washing my hands so that they are clean and clear of any negative energy. I then take both feet in my hands and just hold them for ten to fifteen seconds. This helps me direct my focus to the feet and allows my client to get used to the feeling of my touch. I begin the treatment with the right foot first, and then follow with the left.

Step #1: Take some lotion or oil and warm it in your hands.

Step #2: Gently spread the lotion or oil over the top of the foot and the sole. Concentrate on the sole and work the lotion in so that there's only a light layer remaining. This lets your fingers slide with control!

Step #3: Stimulate all the reflex points on both feet to encourage the entire body to come back into balance. In a whole session, work both feet to treat the entire body. Try to cover every inch of each foot, including the ankle. If you're using this session to handle a specific problem, give more time and attention to the corresponding reflex point. Even so, if time allows working the entirety of both feet, even briefly, it's a good helpmate to wholeness.

Step #4: When you're finished working both feet, I suggest that you wash your hands very well. This serves two purposes: First, it gets rid of any bacteria and dirt that you may have picked up, and second, it literally washes away any negative energy that may have transferred to you during the treatment.

The Approach: How to treat the feet

For each person, the treatment and effect of reflexology are unique. Since no two bodies are the same, every reflexology treatment is different as it is always adjusted to meet the needs of the individual. In this sense, reflexology is holistic and somewhat intuitive. If you only have a few moments to work, I suggest you go right to "problem" areas. If you're working on yourself, you can usually tell where your feet are tender and where you need to focus your attention. If you're working on someone else, the best thing to do is to ask them what part of their body, if any, may be bothering them and start from there. Ask them to let you know if you hit any tender areas so that you can concentrate there. And by all means, don't overlook your instincts when working on yourself or others. If you suddenly feel like you should spend more time on a spot, do so!

On those occasions when you have more time, there are several different ways to treat the feet. Here are a few different techniques:

1. First-aid. Treat specific symptoms: If you (or your partner) are aware of symptoms of stress in your body, you can go directly to the specific corresponding reflex areas to alleviate the symptoms. For example, if you're suffering from a headache, before you work on any other area of the foot, go directly to the big toe to stimulate the reflex area to the brain and ease headache pain. Sometimes this can bring immediate relief. Chapter Five, "Sole-utions," provides an extensive list of common problems and the corresponding reflex areas used to relieve those symptoms and strengthen the body as well. This supports the body in its own healing process.

2. Treat a system. If you know that you (or your partner) are experiencing problems with one particular body system, such as the gastrointestinal or the reproductive system, you can stimulate that whole area on the feet to affect that system in its entirety. With this approach, you may have to work different areas on each foot, since the organs involved in each system may be on different feet. Chapter Three, "Treat Your Feet Sweet," includes explanations of each body system and details the corresponding areas you can work to strengthen them.

3. Full foot workout. To strengthen each and every part of the body, stimulate the entire foot. The methodical way to do this is to use the four horizontal lines that divide the foot into five separate areas, and work one area at a time.

The four horizontal lines that divide the foot are:

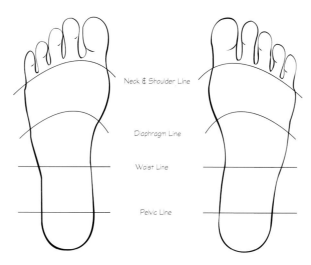

The five vertical lines that divide the foot are:

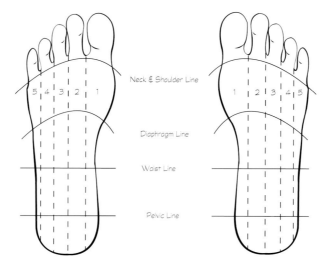

To give the foot a full treatment, begin at the heel of the foot and stimulate the area between the heel and the pelvic line. You can use any of the techniques described in Chapter Three. Next, stimulate the area between the pelvic line and the waist line, then the area between the waist line and the diaphragm line. Move on to stimulate the area between the diaphragm line and the neck and shoulder line, then the area from the neck and shoulder line to the tops of the toes.

As you work on each area, you can feel for "grainy" areas or places where the feet are tender. Rather than going directly to a specific area to try to "fix" a problem, stimulating the entire foot works in the reverse. By discovering grainy or tender areas, you are clued in to energy blockages and potential "problem areas." This allows you to focus on areas of the body that may need the most support, even if you haven't noticed a problem previously.

Working the entire foot has its advantages. Often it is the healthy parts of the body that provide the resources for healing the parts that are ailing or diseased, and when the body uses its own recuperative resources they become strengthened. A benefit of this approach is that you don't need to develop a vast knowledge of human anatomy and physiology in order to be effective. Since the systems, glands, organs, and parts of the body are all so intricately intertwined in their functioning, thorough stimulation of all the reflex areas in your feet can effectively reduce stress and tension, creating a space for healing to occur.

Chapter 3:
Treat Your Feet Sweet

"PLEASURES NEWLY FOUND ARE SWEET WHEN THEY LIE ABOUT OUR FEET."

William Wordsworth

PART I:
HELPFUL HINTS

Now that you understand what reflexology is and the principles behind it, it's time to cut to the rub, if you will. In this chapter, you'll learn easy techniques for stimulating the feet. Don't worry: Reflexology isn't difficult. Like many things it just comes down to a little practice! You don't need to have any previous massage therapy training or an extensive knowledge of anatomy and physiology. All you need are your own two hands and the intention to bring healing to, and through, the feet. Reflexology is so much more than a foot massage. When you touch someone with the intent to bring relaxation and peace, you connect with them on a physical, emotional, mental, and spiritual level. Even if you use the techniques offered in this chapter as a basis for creating your own, as long as you're touching the feet with compassion and tenderness, it can only be good for the sole.

You can choose to use any or all of these reflexology techniques in any order that you feel works best for you. However, you will want to try each once or twice to see which ones are most comfortable and successful for you. As a general rule, however, when focusing on one specific reflex area, it is best to use finger pressure on that point. To stimulate larger areas, such as whole body systems, you can include the techniques that work more of the foot. Reflexology should not hurt and all of the techniques are safe to use. Here are a few things to keep in mind for the most effective reflexology treatment possible.

THINGS TO REMEMBER:

1. Keep your hands soft

Try to keep your hands relaxed and soft when you touch the feet. Remember, the intention of reflexology is to strengthen the body's own healing abilities by relaxing and de-stressing the body. If you can maintain this focus, your touch will convey the energy necessary to clear energy blockages and soothe the body and mind. This is hard to do if your hands irritate the skin!

2. Communicate

If you're working on yourself, you'll know when you hit a sensitive area and you need to lighten your pressure. When you're working on someone else, you'll have to rely on your intuition and good communication to know how to adjust. In the beginning of a treatment, it's important to ask your partner how the pressure you are using feels to them. Tell them to let you know if, at any time, your finger pressure is too hard or painful. Remember, reflexology should feel good. If someone is tensing up because it hurts, much of the positive effect is eliminated.

Take your time and explore as you work. If you come across "grainy" or tender areas, gently work on these areas for several minutes. Usually with a little extra attention, the tenderness disappears.

3. Feel the foot

As you apply the reflexology techniques to the feet, don't forget to tune in to your own sense of touch. The more you practice, the easier it will become to find those areas that feel "grainy."

These are important since they indicate potential problems with the corresponding organ. As you develop more sensitivity in your fingertips, you'll be able to detect subtle changes in the surface of the skin and rub out problems before they manifest in the body. Even if you already know that a specific problem exists, by paying attention to what your fingers are feeling rather than just going through the movements of the technique, you'll be able to give a more effective reflexology treatment.

4. Use your Intuition

As your fingers touch and manipulate the feet, let your intuition be your guide. There is no precise routine for a reflexology treatment, and there are many ways to relieve a problem. The best thing to do if you are giving a full foot treatment is to focus your energy where you sense there is congestion. Although this may seem difficult at first, the more you let your fingers move to where they want, the easier it will be to trust your own intuition. Sometimes, you may feel areas on the foot that are warmer or colder than others. This is a sign of possible congestion in the area. Other times, you may just have a "hunch" to work a certain reflex area. Often, if you ask the person you are working on if they have any problems with the corresponding part of their body, they will confirm your intuition.

5. "Grainy" or Tender Areas

As mentioned previously, after a few practice treatments and as your fingers become more sensitive, you'll be able to detect "grainy" areas on the soles of the feet. These are the crystalline deposits of calcium and uric acid that develop at the base of the nerves when there is an imbalance of energy in the nerve pathway. If you find one, spend several minutes working on this area, trying to break down the crystals. By working on these points you can release blockages and restore the free flow of energy to the whole body.

This may feel tender or even a little painful to the person you are working on. But eventually the graininess disappears and with it, the tenderness and pain also disappear. I always tell people to drink lots of water after a reflexology treatment because the body needs to eliminate the toxins that the reflexology just released from the base of the nerves. A hot bath after a reflexology treatment is also beneficial.

6. Ticklish Feet

The feet are areas of the body that are not often touched, and many people are ticklish when you touch the soles of their feet. Usually, it's a light, feathery touch that makes people squirm, giggle, and instinctively pull their feet away. If someone is ticklish, you can usually get beyond the "squirmy" stage by first holding his foot firmly between both of your hands for about ten seconds. This allows him to get used to the sensations of your touch, and relax. Next, as you begin to stimulate the foot, try to keep the pressure firm and your movements small. The best technique for ticklish people is to simply apply direct pressure with your thumbs on specific reflex areas. If the ticklish person is able to handle thumb pressure, you can add small circles with your thumb moving very slowly. As you feel the foot relax, you can try other reflexology techniques. Just remember to keep your finger pressure firm and your movements slow.

7. Keeping in touch

In a reflexology treatment, there is an exchange of energy between you, the giver, and the receiver (even if the receiver is you). When you begin a treatment and your hands touch the feet, a physical, mental, emotional, and spiritual connection begins. If possible, try to maintain this connection throughout the treatment by always keeping one hand on the feet. Even if you have to take a break, or are interrupted for some reason, just keep "in touch" with one hand. This touch will sustain the energetic exchange so you don't become disconnected with yourself or your partner.

PART II:
REFLEXOLOGY TECHNIQUES

Before you begin a reflexology treatment, take a minute to clear your mind and focus your energy on the intention to bring relaxation and peace. Rub your hands together to create some heat. (There's nothing nice about having someone touch your feet with ice-cold hands!) Take both feet in your hands and just hold them. Take one or two deep breaths, relax, and exhale slowly. Now, you're ready to begin. Work on one foot at a time. Try to stimulate one foot completely and then switch to the other. You may find that you'll need to stimulate different areas on each foot. Or you can do the same routine on both feet. Begin by taking one foot in your hands.

HOLDING THE FOOT

It's important to support the foot properly for the techniques to be as effective as possible. Throughout a reflexology treatment, the hands will be working together in complementary functions. One hand is the "working hand," which is the hand that applies pressure, and the other is the "supporting hand," which braces the foot. If you're right-handed, the right hand would be your working hand. The technique I find most comfortable is placing the supporting hand behind the foot, with fingers on the top of the foot and the thumb on the sole of the foot. This way, the foot is stabilized and you can use your other hand to apply pressure.

ROTATION (ANKLES AND TOES)

I always try to warm the foot up before beginning the deeper, finger pressure techniques. Support the foot by placing one hand under the heel, then use the other hand to slowly rotate the ankle in one direction and then the other. This increases flexibility in the ankle. Next, take each toe between your thumb and index finger and gently roll it back and forth. This relaxing technique wakes up the toes and increases flexibility. It also releases tension in the neck and shoulder area.

ACHILLES TENDON STRETCH

This gentle stretch increases flexibility in the Achilles tendon, which is at the back of the heel, and improves circulation. Support the foot by cupping the heel with one hand. Gently flex the toes backwards and forwards. Next, pull the top of the foot toward you. The heel will move back slightly. Release this stretch and slowly flex the whole foot back and hold it there for two seconds. Repeat this entire process several times to awaken the foot (just as you stretch your arms in the morning to wake up).

SIDE-TO-SIDE ANKLE LOOSENING

This is a technique to relax the ankle and calf muscles, and stimulate circulation. Turn your hands up so that the palms face the ceiling, and place the outer edges of your hands (the "pinkie" sides) on either side of the foot. Gently move your hands left and right, moving up the foot and then down to the heel. The foot should shake from side to side. Do this several times to loosen ankles joints, which reflect the flexibility of all the joints in the entire body. Therefore, a relaxed ankle reflects a relaxed body.

SPINAL TWIST

I like to use this relaxing technique at the beginning of every reflexology treatment, even the five-minute quickies. This technique can relax the entire spine and relieve stress throughout the body. Place both hands side by side on the top of the foot, with the fingers close together and thumbs on the sole of the foot. The hand that is closest to the ankle is the supporting hand, which stabilizes the foot. The hand closer to the toes is the working hand, which moves up the foot towards the toes. The webbing between your thumb and index finger of this hand should lie on the inner edge of the foot, which is the reflex area to the spine. As you move upward, press downward with you fingers so that the foot twists and the webbing of the working hand presses on the inner edge of the foot. Move both hands up toward the toes slightly, and repeat this twisting action.

When you reach the top of the foot, continue the same movement while moving down toward the heel. Stimulating the full length of the inner edge of the foot can relax the entire spine.

KNEADING

This easy relaxation technique is great for improving circulation. Kneading is one technique that requires the use of both hands. Place both hands on either side of the foot, with the thumbs on top and the fingers underneath. Work your fingers into the fleshy part of the sole, as if you are kneading bread. Move your hands up and down the foot. Then you can reverse your hand so that the thumbs are on the bottom. Work your thumbs in a kneading motion up and down the sole.

THUMB-CROSSING

This technique stimulates the bottoms of the feet, and requires both hands. Place the hands on either side of the foot, with the thumbs on the soles and the fingers on the top. Criss-cross your thumbs horizontally across the foot, beginning at the heel and moving up toward the toes and then back down. As your thumbs slide from side to side, apply steady pressure and try to touch the foot from edge to edge.

"V" Thumb Slide

Similar to "thumb-crossing," this technique stimulates the sole of the foot with both hands. Place the hands on either side of the foot, with the thumbs on the soles and the fingers on top. Beginning at the heel, alternate your thumbs as they move outward and upward, from the middle of the foot, at about a 45-degree angle. When you reach the toes, continue this movement back down to the heel.

Solar Plexus Relaxer

The solar plexus is the "nerve switchboard" of the body, and by relaxing its reflex area you can relax the entire body. To locate the solar plexus reflex, hold the top of the foot with the fingers of one hand, and gently squeeze the sides of the foot together so the surface of the sole wrinkles. You'll notice a vertical wrinkle in the center of the foot. At the base of this wrinkle, which is normally at the base of the ball of the foot, lies the solar plexus reflex. Hold the heel with your supporting hand, and press the thumb of your working hand into this area and hold. As your partner inhales, press into the foot, and on the exhalation, release the pressure. Repeat this a couple of times.

To stimulate the solar plexus even deeper, place both thumbs on the solar plexus reflex and gently bend the toes toward you by pressing your fingers downward on the top of the foot. As the foot bends, your thumbs will sink deep into the solar plexus. Release pressure on the exhalation, and apply pressure on the inhalation.

Finger Pressure

Stimulate specific reflex areas on the foot by holding the heel of the foot with one hand and using your thumb to apply steady, static pressure to different points. Hold each reflex area for five seconds and release. Ask your partner to inhale and apply pressure on the inhalation. On the exhalation, release the pressure. You can also make small circles with your thumb on each reflex area. To do this, apply pressure with your thumb, and then keep it in the same spot while moving your hand in a circular motion. Rather than moving the thumb around to "rub" the foot, you're focusing your energy and pressure on one reflex point and almost vibrating or pulsating the point of pressure.

Thumb-walking

This technique allows you to stimulate larger areas on the foot and affect whole body systems, rather than just specific reflex points. Hold the heel with your supporting hand and place your thumb on the reflex area you'd like to affect. Using an "inchworm" movement, bend the thumb at the first joint and inch your thumb up the foot slowly. The walking movement is always forward, never backward. To thumb-walk the entire foot, I recommend dividing the foot into five sections by the horizontal lines (pelvic, waist, diaphragm, and neck/shoulder lines). When you reach the top of a section, bring your thumb back to the line where you started, move the thumb over to the next zone and inch upward. You can cover the entire foot with this technique.

THE ENDING

After you complete a foot treatment, use both hands to "brush" the negative energy out of the foot. Alternating hands, brush your fingertips on the bottom of the foot, from the heel to the toes, and on the top of the foot, from the ankle to the toes. Do this several times on each side of the foot. To end a treatment, place both hands on the feet, and hold them there for a few seconds. This is very relaxing and can enhance the reflexology experience. After you do this, you may want to shake your hands and then wash them with soap and water to get rid of any leftover negative energy. If you're wearing shoes or socks, you may also want to touch the floor with your hands to ground yourself. If you're barefoot, the soles of your feet will "ground" excess energy.

PART III:
FULL FOOT/FULL BODY REFLEXOLOGY ROUTINE

The following routine will guide you through a basic reflexology treatment for the entire foot. You can follow the entire program or you can focus on specific areas of your feet that need particular attention. This routine includes many reflexology techniques, but not all of them. It's up to you to pick and choose the techniques that will work for each situation. As you learn to detect areas of congestion in the feet and to locate specific reflex points, you'll be able to tailor your technique for each person, and give the most effective reflexology session possible.

Step 1: Relax. Before beginning your reflexology session, relax both yourself and the feet by first placing your hands on the top of each foot and then the bottom. Take a deep breath, count to three, and exhale.

Step 2: Stretch. Bring both hands under the heels and pull back, giving a slight stretch to the lower back.

Step 3: Side to side ankle loosening. Move your hands to one foot and place the outer edges of your hands at the heels. Move your hands from side to side to loosen the entire foot.

Step 4: Ankle Rotations. Bring one hand underneath to support the heel, and rotate the ankle in one direction a couple of times, and then the other.

Step 5: Achilles Tendon Stretch. Gently stretch the toes back to release the arch of the foot, and then bring the toes forward, stretching the top of the foot. Next, flex the foot backward and then pull the toes toward you. Repeat this stretch.

Step 6: Solar Plexus Relaxer. Finally, hold both of your thumbs at the solar plexus point, which is in the middle of the foot. This reflex point can relax and calm the entire body.

Step 7: Finger-Walk: neck/shoulder line and up. Beginning at the neck/shoulder line, at the inner edge of the foot, finger-walk up to the top of the toes. Bring your thumb back to the neck/shoulder line, move over to zone 2, and again finger-walk up to the top of the toes. Repeat this in each zone until you reach the outer edge of the foot.

Step 8: Finger-Walk: diaphragm line to neck/shoulder line. Beginning at the diaphragm line, at the inner edge of the foot, finger-walk up to the neck/shoulder line. Bring your thumb back to the diaphragm line, move over to zone 2, and again finger-walk up to the neck/shoulder line. Repeat this in each zone until your reach the outer edge of the foot.

Step 9: Finger-Walk: waist line to diaphragm line. Beginning at the waist line, at the inner edge of the foot, finger-walk up to the diaphragm line. Bring your thumb back to the waist line, move over to zone 2, and again finger-walk up to the diaphragm line. Repeat this in each zone until your reach the outer edge of the foot.

Step 10: Finger-Walk: pelvic line to waist line. Beginning at the pelvic line, at the inner edge of the foot, finger-walk up to the waist line. Bring your thumb back to the pelvic line, move over to zone 2, and again finger-walk up to the waist line. Repeat this in each zone until you reach the outer edge of the foot.

Step 11: Finger-Walk: heel to pelvic line. Beginning at the heel, at the inner edge of the foot, finger-walk up to the pelvic line. Bring your thumb back to the heel, move over to zone 2, and again finger-walk up to the pelvic line. Repeat this in each zone until you reach the outer edge of the foot.

Step 12: Finger-Walk: up the spine. Beginning at the heel, thumb-walk up the inner edge of the foot until you reach the base of the big toe. This stimulates the reflex to the spine and can relax the whole back.

Step 13: Finger Pressure. Apply firm, steady pressure to specific reflex areas that need it the most.

Step 14: Ending. Brush any negative energy out of each foot with alternating hands. Finish by holding the feet.

Part IV:
Reflexology for the Body Systems

Another approach for a reflexology treatment is to focus on one particular body system that may be out of balance and in need of attention. Stimulating all of the body's ten systems can strengthen and balance the system so that it functions as effectively as possible.

1. Circulatory System

The circulatory system consists of the heart, blood vessels, and blood. More than 1,000 times a day, blood circulates in one direction through the body's 60,000-mile network of veins and arteries. The heart is responsible for pumping oxygen into the blood and collecting carbon dioxide that is expelled through the lungs. Approximately 24,000 gallons of blood pass through the heart daily. Red blood cells carry oxygen, minerals, nutrients, hormones, and antibodies to every cell through their 120-day life span, and, along with white blood cells, fight disease. When stress and tension build up in the body, circulation becomes sluggish, the cardiovascular system tightens up, and blow flow is restricted. It's extremely important to manage your stress levels so that the cardiovascular system can conduct a smooth flow of blood throughout the body.

Reflex areas to stimulate:

Heart: Use finger pressure on the heart reflex, located on the left foot.

Blood vessels and blood: Knead, thumb-cross, and "V" slide over the soles of both feet.

2. DIGESTIVE SYSTEM

The digestive system consists of a group of organs that break food down into tiny nutrients so they can be absorbed and converted into energy for the body. This system also builds and replaces cells and tissue. The digestive system begins in the mouth, continues in the pharynx (throat) and esophagus, and extends into the "gut" region, which includes the stomach, the small and large intestines, the rectum, and the anus. As food passes through the body, it is mixed with numerous digestive juices, which break it down into smaller units that can be absorbed into the blood and lymphatic systems. Some are used for energy, some as building blocks for tissues and cells, and some are stored for future or emergency use. The liver and the pancreas also secrete digestive juices that break down food as it passes through the digestive ducts. Since not everything that we eat can be digested, waste is then sent through the colon and out of the body. The digestive system is comprised of the mouth, teeth, tongue, throat, esophagus, stomach, pancreas, duodenum, liver, gall bladder, small intestine, colon, and ileocecal valve.

Reflex areas to stimulate:

Mouth, teeth, tongue, throat, and esophagus: Finger-walk up the entire section between the neck/shoulder line and the tops of the feet. Use finger pressure on the big toe, the reflex to the neck/throat.

Stomach, pancreas, duodenum, liver, gall bladder, small intestine, colon, and ileocecal valve: Thumb-cross and finger-walk up the sections between the pelvic line and the diaphragm line.

3. ENDOCRINE SYSTEM

The endocrine system is a collection of glands that produce the hormones necessary for normal bodily functions. These hormones are responsible for a wide variety of physiological processes, including regulating metabolism, growth, sexual development, emotions, and energy levels. They help the body maintain homeostasis, a state of chemical and emotional balance. The endocrine glands release hormones directly into the bloodstream, where they are transported to organs and tissues throughout the entire body. The endocrine glands regulate the functioning of all the body's systems. The endocrine system is comprised of the hypothalamus, pineal, pituitary, thyroid, parathyroid, thymus, adrenals, pancreas, ovaries in women and testes in men.

Reflex areas to stimulate:

Hypothalamus, pineal, pituitary, thyroid, and parathyroid: Thumb-walk and use finger pressure on the big toe. Work the entire toe, from the base to the top and on both sides.

Thymus, adrenals, and pancreas: Finger-walk the area between the waist line and the diaphragm line.

Ovaries in women and testes in men: Use finger pressure on the area just below the ankle-bone, on the outside of both feet. Add some gentle, circular motion to the finger pressure.

4. LYMPHATIC SYSTEM

The lymphatic system, which is essential to the body's defense mechanisms, filters out organisms that cause disease, produces certain white blood cells, and generates antibodies. It's also important for the distribution of fluids and nutrients in the body, because it drains excess fluids and protein so that tissues do not swell up. The lymphatic vessels are present wherever there are blood vessels, and they transport excess fluid to the end vessels without the assistance of any "pumping" action. The lymphatic system and the cardiovascular system are closely related structures that are joined by a capillary system. The body is able to eliminate the products of cellular breakdown and bacterial invasion through the blood flow, the lymph nodes, and into the lymph.

There are more than one hundred lymph nodes, located mainly in the neck, groin, armpits, and scattered all along the lymph vessels. These act as barriers to infection by filtering out and destroying toxins and germs. The largest body of lymphoid tissue is the spleen. Two significant parts of the lymphatic system are the right lymphatic duct, which drains lymph fluid from the upper right quarter of the body above the diaphragm and down the midline, and the thoracic duct, which drains the rest of the body. It is through the actions of this system that our body is able to fight infection and to ward off foreign invaders. The lymphatic system is comprised of the lymph vessels and ducts, lymph nodes and fluid, spleen, tonsils, thymus, and appendix.

Reflex areas to stimulate:

Lymph vessels and ducts, lymph nodes and fluid: Knead and thumb-cross both feet.
Spleen, tonsils, thymus, and appendix: Use finger pressure on each of these reflex areas.

5. MUSCULAR SYSTEM

The muscular system includes over six hundred muscles of the body. Muscles, which are attached to bones by tendons and other tissues, exert force by converting chemical energy into tension and contraction. They are made up of millions of tiny protein filaments that work together, contracting and releasing, to produce motion in the body. Every single muscle in the body is connected to the brain and spinal cord by nerves. Muscles have many functions, and so we are equipped with three types of muscle: cardiac muscles, found only in the heart, which power the pumping action; smooth muscles, which surround or are part of the internal organs; and skeletal muscles, which are the muscles we use to move our bodies. Cardiac and smooth muscles are involuntary and are not under any conscious control. The skeletal muscles, on the other hand, carry out voluntary movements. They are the body's most abundant tissue, as they comprise about twenty-three percent of a woman's body weight and about forty percent of a man's body weight. The muscular system includes the heart, diaphragm, and intestinal walls.

Reflex areas to stimulate:

600 muscles: Knead and finger-walk the entire foot.
Heart, diaphragm: Use finger pressure on these reflex areas.
Intestinal walls: Finger-walk the area between the pelvic line and the waist line.

6. Nervous System

The central nervous system is the body's information gatherer, storage center, and control system. Its overall function is to collect information about the body's external state, to analyze this information, and to respond appropriately to satisfy certain needs, the most powerful of which is survival. The nerves do not form one single system, but several interrelated systems. The brain and spinal cord make up the central nervous system. The peripheral nervous system is responsible for the body functions that are not under conscious control, such as your heartbeat or digestive system.

The nervous system uses electrical impulses, which travel along the length of the cells. Each cell processes information from the sensory nerves and initiates an action within milliseconds. These impulses travel at speeds up to 250 miles per hour, while other systems, such as the endocrine, may take many hours to respond with hormones. The nervous system is comprised of the brain (including the hypothalamus, pituitary, and pineal glands), spinal cord, and solar plexus.

Reflex areas to stimulate:

Brain (including the hypothalamus, pituitary, and pineal glands): Finger-walk the entire big toe, from the base of the toe to the top, and on both sides.

Spinal cord: Finger-walk along the inside edge of the foot, from the heel to the base of the big toe.

Solar plexus: Use the Solar Plexus Relaxer technique.

7. Reproductive System

The male reproductive system consists of the penis, seminal vesicles, vas deferens, prostate, and testes. This system enables a man to fertilize a woman's eggs with sperm. Sperm, along with male sex hormones, is produced in the testes, a pair of oval-shaped glands that are suspended in a pouch called the scrotum. The male sexual organs are partly visible and partly hidden within the body. The visible parts are the penis and the scrotum. Inside the body are the prostate gland and tubes, which link the system together. The male organs produce and transfer sperm to the female for fertilization.

The female reproductive system consists of the vagina, uterus, fallopian tubes, ovaries, and mammary glands. These organs enable a woman to produce eggs, to nourish and house a fertilized egg until it is fully developed, and to give birth. Unlike the male, the female sexual organs are almost entirely hidden.

Reflex areas to stimulate:

Men: Penis, seminal vesicles, vas deferens, prostate, and testes.

Women: Vagina, uterus, fallopian tubes, ovaries, and mammary glands.

For both men and women, use finger pressure on the inside and outside of each foot, just under the ankle-bone. On each foot, finger-walk along the pathway over the top of the foot that connects the anklebones.

8. Respiratory System

Healthy functioning of the respiratory system is necessary for survival. The respiratory system contains those organs that are responsible for carrying oxygen from the air to the blood stream and expelling the waste product—carbon dioxide. Breathing, like the beat of one's heart, is an automatic function that is controlled by the brain. Respiration is the act of burning energy from oxygen. Breathing is an obvious part of the respiratory flow, but the flow of energy and air is also involved in yawning, sneezing, coughing, hiccuping, speaking, and sensing smell. The respiratory flow is also channeled to the larynx, or voice box, which uses it to create a range of sounds so that humans can communicate vocally. The respiratory system is comprised of the nose, sinuses, lungs, and diaphragm.

Reflex areas to stimulate:

Nose and sinuses: Finger-walk all of the toes. Use finger pressure on the tops of each toe.

Lungs and diaphragm: Finger-walk the area between the diaphragm line and neck/shoulder line.

9. Skeletal System

The average adult human skeleton has 206 bones that store minerals such as calcium, which can be supplied to other parts of the body. The bones are joined to ligaments and tendons to form a protective, supportive framework for the attached muscles and the soft tissues that underlie it. The skeleton plays an important part in movement by providing a series of independently movable levers, which the muscles can pull to move different parts of the body. The skeleton also produces red blood cells from the bone marrow of certain bones, and produces white blood cells from the marrow of other bones to destroy harmful bacteria.

The skeleton consists of the skull, the spine, the ribs, the sternum (breastbone), the shoulders, the pelvis, and their attached limb bones. Babies are born with 270 soft bones—about sixty-four more than adults; many of these fuse together by around the age of twenty into the 206 hard, permanent bones.

Reflex areas to stimulate:

All the bones of the body: Knead and finger-walk the entire foot.

10. Urinary System

The urinary system is a little like a plumbing system, with special pipes that allow water and salts to flow through them. The structure of the urinary tract includes the kidneys, two ureters (tubes leading from the kidneys to the bladder), and the urethra, a tube leading from the bladder to the exterior of the body. The kidneys make up a filter system for the blood, reabsorbing almost ninety-nine percent of the fluid into it, and sending only two to four pints of waste, or urine, into the bladder for storage until it can be disposed of. The kidneys allow the blood to maintain glucose, salts, and minerals after cleansing it of toxins that will be passed out through the urinary tract.

Reflex areas to stimulate:

Kidneys, bladder, ureter tubes, and urethra: Finger-walk the area between the pelvic line and the waist line. Use finger pressure on the reflex area to the kidneys and bladder.

THE IMPORTANCE OF TOUCH

The most important thing to remember while you are giving a reflexology treatment is that as long as your hands are gentle, you can do no wrong. Therefore, even if you don't follow the techniques outlined in this book and you don't know exactly where the reflex points are for specific body parts, you can still give a great foot massage. The main purpose is to touch the feet with the intention to heal and convey peace, love, and compassion.

Skin specifics: The skin is the largest sensory organ of the body and it is the oldest and most sensitive of our organs. A piece of skin the size of a quarter contains more than three million cells, 100 to 340 sweat glands, fifty nerve endings, and three feet of blood vessels! The sense of touch is the first sense to develop in the womb, and it allows you to learn about our environment and to communicate with others. Through touch, you can communicate what you feel and what you love. You can be touchy and be touched. By simply holding a foot in your hands, you can touch the nervous system and create a calming effect. As you learn more about specific reflex areas, this understanding will only enhance your innate ability to heal yourself and others.

Chapter 4:
Knock Your Sox™ Off

"A PRETTY FOOT IS ONE OF THE GREATEST GIFTS OF NATURE."

J.W. Goethe, *Elective Affinities*

PART I:
WHAT'S GOING ON UNDER YOUR FEET

One of the most important aspects of reflexology is that it provides you with an awareness of your body's organs, muscles, structures, and systems. By understanding the function of each part of the body, you can gain insight into the body's complex configuration and appreciate how it functions as a whole.

In the following pages, you'll find essential information on each of the reflex areas that appear on the Reflexology Sox™, as well as several other important reflex areas that are not shown on the Sox™. In each of these explanations you will learn how to locate a specific reflex area, what that body part is exactly, several common physical problems that may be associated with it, and how reflexology can help. In other words, you'll begin discovering how reflexology can help you everyday!

Hint: To make this discovery process more successful as you read each section, try to locate that reflex area on your foot and apply some thumb pressure to it. Spend as much time as you want on each area, but one or two minutes is usually enough. Consider how you felt before and after the pressure was applied. In particular, if you feel any tenderness or "grains of sand" under the skin during this test practice, it may be an indication of an imbalance in that part of the body. I suggest that you then look at Related Problems for that part of the body, located at the end of each section, and turn to the descriptions of those problems in Chapter Five, "Sole-utions".

As you read about the symptoms for specific problems, you may recognize one or two of them. While I always recommend seeking the guidance of a medical doctor if you feel you have a physical problem, stimulating the reflex areas that relate to that problem can often clear up congestion in the pathways and rebalance the energy. The result is that you may feel better quite quickly, or at least minimally, so you can help keep the problem from getting worse.

HOW TO FIND THE REFLEX AREAS ON YOUR FEET

As you read each section, look at the chart of the left and right foot and locate the reflex area that corresponds to the part of the body you would like to affect. Next, locate that reflex area on your own foot. If you have the Reflexology Sox™ on your feet, it's easy. Simply make sure the toes on each sock are lined up with your toes, and the heel of each sock is lined up with your heel. The Reflexology Sox™ are made to stretch so that they fit any foot size. All of the reflex areas should fall into place so you can find the correct area for different parts of your body on your own feet.

Locating specific reflex areas (without Reflexology Sox™)

In order to locate specific reflex areas if you don't have the Reflexology Sox™, it's useful to understand the four lines that divide the foot and the body. Each foot is divided horizontally and vertically into five areas, which correspond to certain areas of the body.

Each foot is also divided into five vertical zones, running from the toes to the heel, which correspond to five zones of the body. You can locate specific reflex points on the foot by studying these divisions and zones and understanding the areas of the body to which they correspond. The area on the feet above the neck and shoulder line corresponds to every part of the body on or above this line, including the head, eyes, ears, brain, and neck. The area above the diaphragm line corresponds to every part of the body between the shoulders and diaphragm, including the chest, heart, lungs and shoulders. The area below the diaphragm line corresponds to organs between the diaphragm and waist, including the upper abdominal organs, spleen, and kidneys. The area between the waist line and pelvic line corresponds to organs below the waist, including the lower abdominal organs, bladder, colon, and intestines. Finally, the area below the pelvic line corresponds to the pelvic area, appendix, sigmoid colon, and sciatic nerve. The inner (medial) edge of the foot corresponds to the spine. And the outer (lateral) edge corresponds to the arm, shoulder, hip, leg, and knee. The ankle corresponds to the pelvic area, including the reproductive organs.

NOW THAT YOU'VE FOUND THE SPOT…

Once you've located "the spot" that is associated with your particular problem, apply some thumb pressure to stimulate the area. You can use any of the techniques from the previous chapter, or make up your own. Spend as much time as you want on each area, but one to two minutes is usually enough. If you feel any tenderness or "grains of sand" under the skin, this may be an indication of an imbalance or weakness in that part of the body. Actually, the graininess is a little deposit of calcium and uric acid that develops at the base of the nerve when there is a problem with a part of the body that is connected to that nerve. Pay extra attention to any tender areas, for these are the reflex areas that need the most help. Reflexology can open up the energy pathways in your body to strengthen it and promote natural healing.

Chakras, Colors, Elements, and Related Problems

At the end of each section, you'll find the chakra, color, and element in traditional Chinese medicine that is associated with that part of the body, as well as several related problems. In brief, you can use this information to combine modalities, like color therapy (surrounding yourself with a healing color for the problem at hand) or elemental balancing (adding an element into your environment) to augment the overall benefits that reflexology provides. For more information on how the chakras and colors relate to your feet, turn to Chapter Six, "Sole Food."

If you recognize any of the related problems listed, you can find more information about them in Chapter Five, and try some of the suggestions given there. Again, please don't overlook the signals that your body and reflexology might be giving you about your health. If you find a problem, seek medical care and use reflexology as a way of maintaining greater balance throughout the treatment process.

PART II:
REFLEX AREAS FOUND ON REFLEXOLOGY SOX™

BLADDER

The reflex to the bladder is located on the inner edge of both feet, below the waist line and above the pelvic line.

What is it?

The bladder, located behind the pubic bone, is a hollow muscular organ that acts as the body's storage area for urine. It's designed to shrink when it is empty, and expand when it's full. An adult bladder can hold approximately 1½ cups of fluid when it's full. Depending on how much liquid is consumed the average adult passes about 1½ quarts of urine every day. That's a lot of trips to the bathroom!

The bladder collects and stores urine until it can be expelled from the body. Although normal urine, which contains excess salts extracted from the blood and nitrogenous toxins such as urea and uric acid, is highly acidic, the bladder itself is shielded from this waste matter by a protective lining. Bladder infections, which are common among women, often occur due to tears or "leaks" in this protective lining which allow toxins from the urine to penetrate and irritate the walls of the bladder.

How can reflexology help?

Stimulating the reflex area to the bladder can strengthen the bladder and the entire urinary tract. This can improve your body's elimination process and balance fluid levels. It also helps prevent bladder infections and those annoying urinary tract infections.

Since the bladder reflex point is associated with the second chakra, the Lower Abdomen chakra, stimulating this spot has the secondary advantage of helping you to open up and really share emotions with others. It can help you feel happy and connected to life.

> Chakra Association: Second chakra, the Lower Abdomen chakra
>
> Color Association: Orange
>
> Element: Water
>
> Related Problems: Acne, bladder infections (interstitial cystitis), kidney problems, prostate problems, urinary tract infections (UTIs)

Brain

The reflex area to the brain is located on both feet, at the base of the ball of the big toe.

What is it?

The brain is a mysterious organ and researchers still don't know everything about what goes on there. The brain itself is a jelly-like substance, which weighs about three pounds in adults. It is divided into three parts including:

1. Brain stem, which regulates the respiratory system, blood pressure, and pulse.

2. Cerebellum, which controls circulation, sleep, and coordinates motor skills.

3. Cerebral cortex, which comprises seventy percent of the brain to control our highest bodily functions and communication skills.

Traditionally referred to as one's "gray matter," the brain's surface contains nerve cell bodies that surround a smaller mass of white nerve fibers. The brain is a fragile organ that is protected by the skull and a surrounding shield of fluid. It provides us with the capacity to think, feel, and survive by regulating and guiding the body's automatic processes such as breathing and digesting. The brain is, in effect, like a complex computer hard drive, and when something goes wrong with it, every system in the body is affected.

How can reflexology help?

Stimulating the reflex to the brain can motivate sensory receptors and help to improve all of your body's systems. Maybe even more importantly, it can bring a sense of calm and peace that can soothe your soul.

The brain reflex point is associated with the seventh chakra, the Crown chakra. Located at the top of the head, it represents your connection with the universe. Stimulating the reflex to the brain can help you let go of fear and anxiety and recognize the interconnectedness and oneness of all living things. It can enhance your spirituality by encouraging your connection with God and/or Spirit.

Chakra Association: Seventh chakra, the Crown chakra

Color Association: White or Gold

Element: Water

Related Problems: Anxiety, chronic fatigue syndrome, constipation, depression, eye problems, headaches, high blood pressure, immunity problems, insomnia, menopause, migraines, multiple sclerosis, nausea, PMS, sex and stress

Colon

The reflex area to the colon is located on both feet, between the waist line and the pelvic line, and it looks like an upside-down U. On the right foot, you'll find the reflex area to the ascending colon in the middle of the foot moving up toward the toes, and the reflex area to part of the transverse colon, which moves across towards the inner edge of the foot. On the left foot, you'll find the reflex area to the rest of the transverse colon, which moves across the foot toward the outer edge, and the reflex area to the descending colon, which moves down toward the heel. It is best to work the right foot first, beginning at the base of the ascending colon and moving up and across the transverse colon. To work the left foot, begin at the inner edge of the transverse colon and move towards the outer edge and then down the descending colon to the sigmoid colon.

What is it?

The colon, or bowel, is a tube-like organ that assists in the elimination of waste products. It's the last and widest section of the digestive tract. When stretched out, it is approximately five to six feet long. In the colon, undigested pieces of food are compacted, water is reabsorbed into the body, and waste is stored in the rectum until it is eliminated. Normally, a healthy colon will take between sixteen and eighteen hours to process a meal and eliminate it from the body. When it takes longer that this, you may be constipated and may feel sluggish due to the toxins in the waste that is still in your system. On the other hand, when you eliminate too quickly, such as when you have diarrhea, your body may not absorb enough nutrients and you can become dehydrated and mineral-deficient.

The colon has an inner lining of epithelium cells that is particularly susceptible to the development of colon polyps, which occur in thirty to forty percent of older Americans. Although colon polyps, also known as *adenomas*, are not the same as malignant colon cancer, if they are present for long periods of time they may become cancerous. Unfortunately, it is still a mystery as to what exactly causes colon cancer, a disease with alarmingly increasing rates each year. In the United States, men and women are equally affected by this disease, with an annual diagnosis of about 160,000 people, of which 60,000 cases are terminal.

More common still, and less tragic, many people suffer from cramps caused by gas that is trapped in one part of the colon. To prevent gas and waste buildup in this area, you can stimulate the reflex area to this part of the colon, which is located on the left foot, at the end of the descending colon.

How can reflexology help?

Stimulating the reflex area to the colon can help to encourage healthy elimination of waste from the body and possibly prevent many diseases of the colon. In addition, it can help to relieve gas, constipation, and cramps, which almost everybody suffers from at one time or another.

The colon reflex point corresponds with the first chakra, the Root chakra, which helps you feel "grounded" on the Earth. Stimulating the reflex area that corresponds to the colon can help you trust in the laws of nature. In other words, trust that there is a reason for everything and you will be able to provide for yourself. This chakra is related to your feelings of security in life.

> Chakra Association: First chakra, the Root chakra
>
> Color Association: Red
>
> Element: Earth
>
> Related Problems: Colon problems, constipation, diarrhea, Crohn's disease, diverticulosis/diverticulitis, hemorrhoids, irritable bowel syndrome (IBS), ulcerative colitis

EARS

The reflex area to the ears is located on both feet, in the area just below the base of the pinkie and fourth toes.

What are they?

The ears are complex sensory organs that have as many reflexes as the feet. Like the hands and the feet, the outer ear has reflexes for the entire body. The inner ear allows us to hear sounds. As sound vibrations enter the ear through the ear canal, impulses travel to the brain to be interpreted as sound. At the bottom of the ear canal lies the corti, an organ with 12,000 outer and 3,500 inner sound-sensitive hair cells. Pressure changes in the ear canal cause the hairs to bend and move, and this stimulates a nerve signal, which is carried to the brain by the cochlear nerve. Some sounds at particular frequencies make more vibrations than others, stimulating a specific group of hair cells so that the sound can be recognized.

The second, larger part of the inner ear has nothing to do with hearing. It is a series of fluid-filled chambers and ducts, containing more hair cells, which activate eye and body muscles when you turn your head. These hair cells also sense the direction of gravity and straight-line movements, coordinate eye and head movements, and control your sense of balance. Since humans have only two legs and balance is often unstable, continuous adjustments must be applied so that we do not fall over.

> Fun fact: Many people believe that when you put your ear up to a seashell, you can hear the sounds of the ocean. Actually, what you hear is an echo of the pulse in your own head.

How can reflexology help?

Stimulating the reflex areas to the ears can reduce pressure in the ear and open passageways, which is quite helpful for allergy and sinus sufferers. It can help also to relieve vertigo and the symptoms of dizziness and nausea that often accompany it.

The ear reflex points are associated with the sixth chakra, the Third Eye chakra, which is related to our connection with a higher consciousness. Stimulating the reflex area to the ears can help you hear the call of the universe so that you may experience knowledge that is beyond words or intellect. It can also increase your intuition and perception in everyday life.

Chakra Association: Sixth chakra, the Third Eye chakra

Color Association: Purple

Element: Fire

Related Problems: Ear problems, motion sickness, nausea

EYES

The reflex area to the eyes is located on both feet, in the area just below the second and third toes.

What are they?

As "windows to the soul," the eyes are our sensory organs for vision. Although the eyes are at the front of the head, our visual sense comes from areas of the brain at the back and sides. If the eye were a camera, the retina would be the camera's film. When light rays reach the retina, light energy is converted into electrical nerve signals that travel to the brain and become images that we can understand. These nerve signals are generated by photoreceptors called rods and cones in the retinas of the eyes. Rods are sensitive enough to respond to a single photon, the basic unit of light, but they are only able to create one coarse, gray image, which is only adequate for seeing in poor light. Cones, on the other hand, need more light but are able to pick up fine detail and color. Inside the human eye, there are eighteen times more rods than cones. These are arranged to produce the best possible combination of night and day vision.

How can reflexology help?

Stimulating the reflex area to the eyes on both feet can help improve the overall condition of the eyes and help relieve annoying eye problems. It allows you to see the world more clearly and brings everything into focus.

The eye reflex points are associated with the sixth chakra, the Third Eye chakra, which is related to your senses of intuition and perception. Stimulate this reflex area to bring an awareness of things that go beyond concrete reality and touch on the eternal. Opening your Third Eye can help you see and comprehend the truth in what is going on around you more clearly and intuitively.

Chakra Association: Sixth chakra, the Third Eye chakra

Color Association: Purple

Element: Earth

Related Problems: Allergies, eye problems, headaches, migraines, motion sickness

HEART

The reflex to the heart is located on the left foot only, closer to the outer edge and above the waist line.

What is it?

The heart's main function is to be a pump for the blood. A good majority of the heart consists of a special type of muscle that works like a pump and contracts automatically to send blood to the lungs and the rest of the body. The heart is made up of four chambers and two separate pumps that work in conjunction with each other. The right side of the heart collects oxygen-poor blood from the veins and pumps it into the lungs, where the body picks up inhaled oxygen and releases carbon dioxide to be exhaled. The oxygen-rich blood is returned to the left side of the heart and then pumped out to the rest of the body. The heart begins the cycle all over again and fills with blood once more. Each time the valves slap shut to prevent the blood's backflow, they make a noise which is the beating sound we hear.

How can reflexology help?

By working the reflex to the heart you can effectively improve the circulation of blood and oxygen in the body. This can strengthen every organ in the body.

The heart reflex point is associated with the fourth chakra, the Heart chakra, which is the center of the chakra system, and governs feelings and emotions. The ability to love freely and unselfishly without fear or expectation is generated from this chakra. Stimulating this reflex area can help you to feel a sense of wholeness, nurture loving relationships, and improve your ability to accept love from others. By opening the heart chakra you can feel love more deeply and express your emotions more freely.

Chakra Association: Fourth chakra, the Heart chakra

Color Association: Green

Element: Fire

Related Problems: Anemia, depression, heart problems, high blood pressure

HEMORRHOIDS

The reflex area for hemorrhoids is located at the base of the heels of both feet. This is the reflex area for the rectum and lower colon area.

What are they?

Hemorrhoids, a painful problem for many people (especially pregnant women), are distended, varicose veins in the rectum that can become inflamed and cause itching, pain, and rectal bleeding. Besides pregnancy, hemorrhoids can be caused by prolonged sitting, constipation, or irritating food in your diet, such as coffee, alcohol, strong spices, and hot or peppery foods. Unfortunately, hemorrhoids will happen to almost everyone at some point in their lives.

How can reflexology help?

Stimulating this reflex area can relax the rectum and relieve the embarrassing and often unbearable discomfort of hemorrhoids. It also soothes pain and promotes healing. Hemorrhoid reflex points are associated with the first chakra, the Root chakra, which relates to the Earth and good foundations. Stimulating this point increases energy, ambition, and the sense of security and feeling at home. Clearing energy in the Root chakra can help you learn to "let go" and trust that the universe will provide for you.

Chakra Association: First chakra, the Root chakra

Color Association: Red

Element: Water

Related Problems: Hemorrhoid problems

HIPS

The reflex area to the hips is located on the outer edge of both feet, below the waist line and the pelvic line.

What is it?

The hips are major weight-bearing joints. Hip pain can be among the more serious indicators of substantial orthopedic problems. Fortunately, most people who complain about hip pain just experience discomfort on the outside of their thigh or buttock region. Pain that is felt in the groin area, however, is an indicator of possible hip problems and should be investigated.

In athletes, bursitis and tendonitis in the hip region are very common. In the more elderly, hip fractures and arthritis are extremely common. Arthritis in the hips can cause extreme pain and limping, increasing limitation of motion and activities. Today, surgeons can replace the entire hip with a ball-and-socket joint made from metal and plastic and engineered in such a way that it will duplicate the motions of a human joint. They have now perfected hip replacements so that recipients are relieved of pain and can walk at a smoother pace.

How can reflexology help?

Stimulating the reflex area to the hips can help to relieve pain in the hips and improve your range of motion. It can also help you walk more easily!

The hip reflex points are associated with the second chakra, the Lower Abdomen chakra, which is the center for sexual energy, creativity, and emotions. Stimulating this chakra encourages the exchange of feelings in relationships in new and innovative ways, especially where communications have been difficult. The hips are a huge storage area for emotional baggage, so clearing the energy in this chakra can help you process emotions and rid the body of them before they become damaging.

> Chakra Association: Second chakra, the Lower Abdomen chakra
>
> Color Association: Orange
>
> Element: Wood
>
> Related Problems: Arthritis, sciatica, tendonitis

KIDNEYS

The reflex area to the kidneys is located on both feet, running through the waist line, in the middle of the foot but slightly closer to the inner edges.

What are they?

The kidneys, shaped like a kidney bean and located about two inches above the body's midline just below and behind the liver in the upper abdomen and behind the lower ribs, are the body's own "filter treatment plant." About one-quarter (750–1,000 pints daily) of the blood that is output by the heart is sent to the kidneys, where it is purified and circulated throughout the rest of the body.

The kidneys balance our internal fluids; if we eat or drink too much, or sweat a lot and don't drink enough, the kidneys will compensate to make sure that fluctuations in fluid, salt, and glucose are leveled out. They balance the body's acid/alkaline nature and the concentrations of salts and minerals. Kidneys are quite strong. In fact, less than half of one single kidney can do all the work that two kidneys usually do. This is why kidney transplants are possible, and kidney donors can safely give one kidney away with minimal risk to their own health.

How can reflexology help?

By working the reflex to the kidneys, you can help promote balanced elimination of the body's water and waste. You can strengthen the kidneys and the entire urinary system. Finding grittiness or tenderness in this area could be a sign of kidney stones or other kidney-related problems. You prevent these problems by balancing the energy to the kidneys and encouraging natural healing.

The kidney reflex points are associated with the third chakra, the Solar Plexus chakra, which is related to your sense of power. This chakra is where your personality is formed. Stimulating this reflex area can promote a sense of inner peace and happiness with the self, and in turn nurture a feeling of tolerance and acceptance of others.

Chakra Association: Third chakra, the Solar Plexus chakra

Color Association: Yellow

Element: Water

Related Problems: Acne, arthritis, bladder infections, diarrhea, eye problems, hangovers, kidney problems, psoriasis, urinary tract infections (UTIs)

LIVER

The reflex area to the liver is located on the outer edge of the right foot only, running through and just above the waist line.

What is it?

The liver, the "great filter of the body," is an extremely important organ and has multiple functions, one of which is to make the important decision as to whether incoming substances are useful to the body or whether they are waste. The liver is responsible for detoxifying the blood and processing nutrients. It breaks down fatty acids and converts glucose to a storage-form of energy called glycogen. The liver also produces glucose from substances other than sugars and starches such as proteins. It receives bright red blood from the lungs, filled with vital oxygen to be delivered to the heart. When we eat, more blood is sent to the intestines to deal with digestive processes. When we're not eating, three-fourths of the blood supply to the liver comes from the intestines. The liver also produces about two and one-half pints of bile, which is delivered to the gall bladder. The liver is located at the top of the abdomen, just below the diaphragm. It is the largest gland in the body, weighing 2.5 to 3.3 pounds in adults. In one minute, it receives thirty percent of the blood that is pumped through the heart. The only part of the body that receives more blood than the liver is the brain.

How can reflexology help?

Stimulating the reflex area to the liver can help detoxify your blood and encourage your body to absorb as many nutrients and iron as possible from the blood. This can help your entire digestive system to function better.

The liver reflex points are associated with the third chakra, the Solar Plexus chakra, which is located in the center of the body. It relates to your sense of personal strength, fortitude, and feeling whole. Stimulating the reflex area to the liver, therefore, provides self-empowerment.

Chakra Association: Third chakra, the Solar Plexus chakra

Color Association: Yellow

Element: Wood

Related Problems: Acne, anemia, asthma, arthritis, hangovers, kidney problems,
psoriasis, urinary tract infections (UTIs)

Lungs

The reflex area to the lungs is located on both feet, above the waist line and below the second
and third toes, in the middle of the foot.

What are they?

The body's respiratory system is mainly contained in the right and left lung. Together, they
are the body's largest organs. They weigh less than two pounds, but they can hold about $1\frac{1}{2}$
gallons of air. The lungs are the organs responsible for oxygenating the body by exchanging new,
inhaled oxygen with old, used de-oxygenated carbon dioxide. The lungs are like an upside-
down tree with many branches. The right lung is made up of three compartments with "twigs"
that hold numerous air sacs (or "fruit" of the tree). These air sacs have thin walls that allow gases
to pass in and out.

The passageways in the sacs are lined with various types of epithelia cells to prepare the air
properly for utilization, and with hair-like fibers called cilia that move in a wave-like motion to
sweep debris out of the lungs. They process the oxygen in the air that will be released into the
blood and expel carbon dioxide, which is exhaled through the nose and mouth. The left lung cavity contains only two sections (each with its own branches, twigs, and fruit) and encloses the heart.

The lungs bring life to the body and can help relax and de-stress all of your systems. When
you're anxious, breathing tends to be shallow and short. You take more breaths per minute and
suck air mainly into the upper chest. To relax, deep breathing all the way into the belly can
help. Try to inhale as much oxygen as possible, filling the lungs completely from the bottom
upward with slow, long breaths. Concentrating on full inhalations and exhalations for just a few
minutes can calm your body and mind.

How can reflexology help?

Work the reflex areas to the lungs on both feet to strengthen the respiratory system and
improve breathing. This can promote healthy oxygenation of the blood, which will improve
your overall well-being.

The lung reflex points are associated with the fourth chakra, the Heart chakra, which relates
to feelings of love, forgiveness, compassion, hope, and trust. This chakra neutralizes negative
emotions and feelings and encourages the free exchange of positive emotion.

Chakra Association: Fourth chakra, the Heart chakra

Color Association: Green

Element: Metal

Related Problems: Acne, anemia, asthma, arthritis, hangovers, kidney problems,
psoriasis, urinary tract infections (UTIs)

NECK

The reflex area to the neck is located at the base of the big toe on both feet, along the neckline.

What is it?

The neck is a complex and vulnerable area of the body that is comprised of seven "cervical vertebrae," which make up the beginning of the spine, and numerous muscles and delicate nerves. Many parts of the neck are not easily accessible, which makes reflexology an ideal therapy for minor aches and pains in this area. Two of the cervical vertebrae are of special interest. The first vertebra (also called the "atlas") supports and balances the head. Like the mythological god, Atlas, who held up the world, the atlas holds up our head. It has practically no body or spine and appears as a bony ring with two kidney-shaped facets that connect with the occipital ridge of the skull. The second vertebra is the "axis," which projects upward and lies in the ring of the atlas. As the head turns from side to side, the axis pivots around the atlas.

The neck contains many muscles, ligaments, arteries, and nerves that are vulnerable to damage. The *common carotid artery* carries much of the blood supply to the head, and the *carotid sinus* is equipped with sensory nerves that measure blood supply pressure in order to maintain appropriate blood flow to the head. If these nerves are damaged or if external pressure is applied to these arteries, it can lead to dizziness and fainting. At the back of the neck, there are nerves about the size of shoelaces that interweave with each other and wrap around the muscles of the shoulder and arm. These nerves sometimes get blocked against several different tissues or bones on the way to the arm, which leads to intense neck pain that can radiate all the way down the arm.

How can reflexology help?

Pain and stiffness in the neck are common complaints. Reflexology can help relieve the pressure and discomfort in a part of the body that is difficult, if not impossible, to reach, especially by yourself.

The neck reflex points are associated with the fifth chakra, the Throat chakra, which is related to communication and creativity. This chakra deals with transforming feelings and emotions into physical expressions such as laughter or crying. Stimulate this area to strengthen your ability to listen to your inner voice and to express your true feelings and thoughts.

> Chakra Association: Fifth chakra, the Throat chakra
>
> Color Association: Blue
>
> Element: Water
>
> Related Problems: Back problems, ear problems, headaches, heartburn and indigestion, hernias, neck pain, migraines, thyroid problems

SCIATIC NERVE

The sciatic nerve area for reflexology is located on both feet, running across the heel of the foot. This is not a reflex area, but rather the actual nerve that runs from the base of the heel, up the leg, and into the buttocks.

What is it?

The sciatic nerve is the largest and longest nerve in the body. In a band about as thick as your thumb (or about .8 inches across), the sciatic nerve branches from the lumbar (lower back) nerves in the sacrum, and descends into each buttock, through the deep lateral rotators, and down into the thighs where they divide just above the knees, into the *tibial* and *common peroneal* nerves. These nerves continue all the way down the lower leg and end on the soles of both feet. The sciatic nerve supplies impulses to and from the muscles and tissues in the hip joints and thighs, the lower legs, feet, and most of the area below the knee.

Sciatica is a common problem that affects the sciatic nerve. Often caused by vertebrae pressing on or pinching the nerve, sciatica can cause a sharp, stabbing pain that radiates from the buttocks all the way down the leg to the foot. Sciatica is common in pregnant women and people who sit in one position, usually with their legs crossed, for long periods of time. Stretching and massage of the sciatic nerve can be extremely helpful.

For clients who suffer from sciatica, I often recommend placing a tennis ball under their affected buttock and lying with their back on the floor. The weight of the body will help the ball sink deep into the muscle and can relieve the pain caused by a pinched sciatic nerve.

How can reflexology help?

When the sciatic nerve becomes inflamed and irritated, the pain that runs down the legs can be excruciating and often debilitating. Since the sciatic nerve continues into the heel of the foot, stimulating the base of the nerve can be extremely effective in relaxing the entire leg and relieving pain.

The sciatic nerve reflex point is associated with the second chakra, the Lower Abdomen chakra, which is your center for sexual energy, creativity, and pure emotions. Stimulate this area to improve physical pleasure, release creativity, and prevent repressed sexuality.

> Chakra Association: Second chakra, the Lower Abdomen chakra
>
> Color Association: Orange
>
> Element: Water
>
> Related Problems: Sciatica, numbness in the feet

SHOULDERS

The reflex area to the shoulders is located on both feet, on the outer edge of the foot below the pinkie toe.

What is it?

The shoulder is made up of two separate joints; it is located where the bone of the upper arm, or *humerus*, meets the shoulder blade, or *scapula*, and where the clavicle meets the scapula. The shoulder joint is a ball-and-socket joint and the most freely moveable joint in the body. Unfortunately, although both joints are held together by extensive ligament and muscle attachments, the shoulder lacks stability and is one of the weakest areas of the body. The shoulder joint is vulnerable to dislocations from sudden jerks of the arm, especially in children whose muscles have not yet developed. Dislocation of the shoulder is extremely painful and may require surgical repair or even cause permanent damage.

How can reflexology help?

The shoulder area is a part of the body that is quite difficult to reach on your own. Stimulating the shoulders' reflex area on your feet can help to relieve aches and pains that most people could never reach on their own. It can help loosen tight muscles and de-stress your entire upper body.

The shoulder reflex point is associated with the fourth chakra, the Heart chakra, which is related to matters of love, forgiveness, compassion, and trust. Many people hold emotional tension and stress in their shoulders. Stimulate this reflex area to release those stressful emotions and help to love more openly and freely.

> Chakra Association: Fourth chakra, the Heart chakra
>
> Color Association: Green
>
> Element: Fire
>
> Related Problems: Back pain, neck pain, headaches, migraines

SINUSES

The toes correspond to the entire head and neck, and the reflex area for the sinuses is located on both feet, at the tips of each of the toes. The sinuses are located in the skull, above and to the sides of the nose, in the cheekbones and behind the eyebrows.

What are they?

The sinuses are cavities in the skull that allow air to pass through. They serve to lighten the skull and also add resonance to your voice. When the sinuses become blocked by swelling and inflammation, pressure builds in the air passageways and can cause extreme pain. Anyone who suffers from sinus headaches, sinusitis, or allergies can tell you that these problems often make you feel as if your head is going to explode! To reduce swelling and restore proper drainage to the sinuses, medications that restrict the blood vessels are often prescribed.

How can reflexology help?

Reflexology is the drug-free way to clear nasal passageways so you can breathe normally again. The easiest way to work the sinuses is to simply pinch the tips of each toe; this can help to clear congested or clogged sinus passages. I have many clients who suffer from terrible sinus problems due to allergies and I have a little trick that works extremely well for them. When allergy season hits and they complain of feeling "stuffed-up" with pressure in their sinuses, I place a clothespin (the wooden, spring-kind that pinch) on the tip of each toe for five minutes while they lie back and relax. The constant pressure from the clothespins for just a few minutes has actually opened up their sinuses so they feel an improvement right away. This technique can be used almost anywhere, including on planes, at work, in front on the TV. Some clients now even travel with clothespins in case allergies hit!

The sinuses' reflex points are associated with the sixth chakra, the Third Eye chakra, which relates to the awareness of a spiritual realm. This chakra helps you strengthen your powers of intuition and perception so that you can connect with your higher self. Opening the Third Eye can also clear your mind in order to see the truth in everything.

Chakra Association: Sixth chakra, the Third Eye chakra

Color Association: Purple

Element: Earth

Related Problems: Allergies, sinus problems, headaches

SMALL INTESTINE

The reflex area to the small intestine is located on both feet, in the area between the waist line and the pelvic line, in the middle of the foot.

What is it?

The small intestine consists of a three-part tube, about 1.5 to 2 inches in diameter, which is responsible for processing about 2.5 gallons of food, liquids, and bodily waste every day. Held in place by tissues that are attached to the abdominal wall, it measures eighteen to twenty-three feet in the average adult, almost four times longer than your height! If the small intestine were not wound around itself, it could not fit into the abdominal space it inhabits.

The small intestine is divided into three sections including:

- the duodenum, which is a receiving area for chemicals and partially digested food from the stomach

- the jejunum, where most of the nutrients are absorbed into the blood

- the ileum, where the remaining nutrients are absorbed before moving into the large intestine

These three sections work together to help the body process food and absorb nutrients by producing large numbers of intestinal cells. Each of these cells contain thousands of tiny finger-shaped projections called *villi*, which bring in fresh, oxygenated blood and send out nutrient-enriched blood. The villi constantly sway back and forth to stir up liquefied food and extract nutrients. The nutrients are absorbed and then passed through the membranes of the villi into the blood and lymph vessels.

The small intestine is surrounded by muscles, which contract about seven to twelve times a minute, that move the food back and forth and mix it with gastric juices. The small intestine itself also makes waves that move the food forward, but these are usually weak and infrequent. However, if a toxic substance enters the small intestine, these movements can become forceful and rapid enough to expel the toxins from the body quickly. That's what happens when you throw up.

How can reflexology help?

Stimulating the reflex area to the small intestine can help strengthen your entire digestive system and improve the body's absorption of nutrients. It can relieve problems such as constipation that cause retention and accumulation of toxic wastes in the tissues. It can increase the body's peristaltic action, which encourages proper elimination of waste matter, relieve stomachaches and cramps, and revive a sluggish metabolism. The small intestine reflex points are associated with the first chakra, the Root chakra, which is related to your sense of having one foot on the ground. In other words, you're not up in the clouds in fantasyland.

Chakra Association: Second chakra, the Lower Abdomen chakra

Color Association: Orange

Element: Fire

Related Problems: Acne, constipation, colon problems, diarrhea, liver problems, nausea, psoriasis

SOLAR PLEXUS

The reflex area to the solar plexus is located on both feet, in the center of the foot just beneath the diaphragm line. Within the body, the solar plexus is situated behind the stomach and in front of the diaphragm.

What is it?

The solar plexus, also called the nerve switchboard of the body, is a network in the abdominal cavity that sends energy impulses to the upper middle part of the abdomen. Its purpose is to help balance the sympathetic nervous system, regulate the functions of the organs, and restore calm. The solar plexus has been called the abdominal brain because it influences the nerves in the abdomen. It's often affected by stress, anger, and depression.

How can reflexology help?

Stimulating the reflex to the solar plexus can relax the entire body and bring overall stress relief. It also promotes better, deeper breathing, and relieves the discomfort of allergies, asthma, and even acne.

Located in the center of the body, the solar plexus reflex point is the center of the third chakra, the Solar Plexus chakra, which relates to your personal power. This chakra is where the personality is formed. Stimulate this area to better express your individuality and strength.

Chakra Association: Third chakra, the Solar Plexus chakra

Color Association: Yellow

Element: Earth

Related Problems: Anxiety, asthma, autoimmune problems, colon problems, chronic fatigue syndrome, ear problems, hangovers, headaches, heartburn and indigestion, high blood pressure, insomnia, menopause, migraines, PMS, sex and stress, thyroid problems

SPINE

The reflex area to the spine is located on each foot, along the entire inside edge, from the base of the big toenail to the base of the heel. This reflex area corresponds to the spine's vertebrae. The seven cervical vertebrae begin at the base of the big toenail and run along the inner edge to the base of the big toe. The twelve thoracic vertebrae follow from the base of the big toe, along the ball of the foot, to the arch near the waist line. The five lumbar vertebrae begin at the waist line and extend to the pelvic line. The five sacral vertebrae and the four coccygeal vertebrae (the "tail") correspond to the area along the inside edge between the pelvic line and the heel.

What is it?

The spine, which consists of a column of bone and cartilage, extends from the base of the skull to the pelvis, and is the central support of the body. It supports the trunk of the body and the head, and encloses and protects the spinal cord, which is a column of nerve tracts running from every area of the body to the brain. There are thirty-one pairs of spinal nerves that originate from the spinal cord and provide a two-way communication system between the spinal cord and parts of the arms, legs, neck, and trunk of the body. Because it houses the body's inner wiring system of nerves, the spine is part of the nervous system and is affected by stress and emotional disturbances.

The spine is composed of approximately thirty-three bones called vertebrae, connected by a joint to the spine. Occasionally, the spine goes out of alignment due to injury or simply by twisting, moving, or even sleeping in an awkward position. When this happens, the electrical impulses that run through certain vertebra may be pinched or cut off. As a result, the associated organ does not receive adequate blood supply and oxygen that it needs for nourishment and proper functioning. This can lead to symptoms that range from discomfort or pain to numbness or muscle spasms. Reflexology, as well as massage of all the muscles of the back, can relieve this common problem.

How can reflexology help?

The spine is often one of the most stressed areas of the body. Unfortunately, it is not an easy area to reach and people sometimes get more stressed when they try to twist their arms around to touch the exact spot where it hurts. Reflexology offers a way to affect parts of your spine that you could never reach yourself. By stimulating the corresponding reflex area on the inside of each foot, you can soothe specific areas along your spine. Got an ache in the middle of your back? Stimulate the middle area of the inside edge of your foot.

The spine reflex area runs along the pathway of the chakra system. Therefore, the spine is associated with the entire energy pathway. Beginning with the base of the spine, which corresponds to the first chakra, the Root chakra, you can follow all the way up to the top of the neck, which corresponds to the fifth chakra, the Throat chakra. Stimulating the reflex to the spine can encourage energy to spiral up the spine and into the sixth chakra, the Third Eye. This can balance all of the energy centers of the body and promote a sense of calm.

> Chakra Association: First chakra (Root chakra) to the Fifth chakra (the Throat chakra)
>
> Color Association: Red, Orange, Yellow, Green, Blue
>
> Element: Water
>
> Related Problems: Anxiety, back problems, neck pain, headaches, kidney problems, multiple sclerosis

Spleen

The reflex to the spleen is located on the outer edge of the left foot, just under the pad of the little toe, near the heart reflex. You can find it in line with the fourth toe, below the diaphragm.

What is it?

The spleen is a large, gland-like organ that is part of the lymphatic system. Located on the left side of the body, just behind the stomach, the spleen is about the size of the heart, which makes it the largest of the lymphoid tissues, and consists of a spongy material which holds up to .3 gallons of blood. The spleen stores and filters the blood, produces some of the white blood cells, destroys old, worn-out red blood cells, produces antibodies, and returns needed iron to the blood, disposing of the rest. It's also responsible for storing excess blood for emergencies when oxygen in the circulatory system is short. Since the spleen is so soft and spongy, it cannot be repaired by surgery. Thus, if it is ever ruptured, it is usually removed to stop the loss of blood.

How can reflexology help?

Stimulating the reflex to the spleen can help purify the blood and balance blood deficiencies. It opens channels of energy that can encourage natural healing and better health of this organ.

The spleen reflex point is associated with the third chakra, the Solar Plexus chakra, which is related to your center of personal power. Stimulate this region to learn how to accept yourself and your talents more readily.

> Chakra Association: Third chakra, the Solar Plexus chakra
>
> Color Association: Yellow
>
> Element: Earth
>
> Related Problems: Anemia, immunity problems, inflammation

STOMACH

The reflex area to the stomach is located on both feet, but mainly on the left foot, under the diaphragm line and above the pelvic line.

What is it?

The stomach is a hollow, sac-like organ, connected to the esophagus and the duodenum (the first part of the small intestine), that produces gastric juices, which break down protein and help the body to process food. It is also a storage compartment, which allows us to eat only two or three meals a day. Without a stomach to hold food, we would have to eat about every twenty minutes! The average adult stomach stretches to hold from four to six cups of food and it produces approximately the same amount of gastric juices every twenty-four hours.

The stomach has several functions besides storage and digestion. It also blends foods and sterilizes germs that are found in those foods. Normally, the stomach is prepared to go to work when food arrives because the digestive process is triggered by the sight, smell, or taste of food. Every time you smell something really delicious, your body begins digesting. Problems such as painful ulcers may arise when the stomach is not filled up and gastric juices begin eroding the stomach lining itself. So go ahead and fill that stomach!

How can reflexology help?

Working the stomach reflex areas can improve digestion and encourage muscular activity within the abdomen. This can soothe tummy aches, ulcers, and cramps, and relieve anxiety-caused "butterflies."

The stomach reflex area is associated with the third chakra, the Solar Plexus chakra, which relates to your sense of centering and energy. Stimulate this chakra to strengthen your personal power.

Chakra Association: Third chakra, the Solar Plexus chakra

Color Association: Yellow

Element: Earth

Related Problems: Anxiety, constipation, colon problems, diarrhea, hangovers, heartburn and indigestion, hernias, migraines, motion sickness, nausea, PMS, ulcers

THYMUS

The reflex area to the thymus is located on both feet, below the neckline and above the diaphragm line.

What is it?

The thymus is a lymphatic gland, located in the upper part of the chest, above and in front of the heart, which forms part of the immune system. Its primary responsibility is to build this system by transforming white blood cells developed in the bone marrow into T-cells. These T-cells are then transported to various lymph glands, where they play an important part in fighting infection and disease. Often, swelling of the lymph glands and an accompanying fever are a signal that immune cells are multiplying to fight off invaders of the body such bacteria, fungi, viruses, or parasites.

The thymus grows from about the twelfth week of gestation until puberty. It is larger when we are young children because it is working harder to develop an immune system that can fight disease effectively. This gland actually begins to shrink after puberty and almost disappears as we get older.

How can reflexology help?

Stimulating the reflex area to the thymus gland can help boost your immune system, which may be compromised during allergy season, and invigorates your body, which can feel "zapped" of energy. Working this area on children encourages the development of a strong, healthy immune system.

The thymus gland reflex point is associated with the fourth chakra, the Heart chakra, which is related to feelings of wholeness and love. Stimulating this chakra opens your heart to allow you to express and feel emotions more deeply.

Chakra Association: Fourth chakra, the Heart chakra

Color Association: Green

Element: Earth

Related Problems: Allergies, asthma, autoimmune problems, ear problems, eye problems, immunity problems, inflammation, kidney problems, multiple sclerosis, low sex drive, ulcers

Thyroid (Parathyroids)

The reflex area to the thyroid is situated on both feet, just below the base of the big toe, around the ball of the foot, and into the crease below the bone.

What is it?

The thyroid gland, located just below your Adam's apple, regulates the state of chemical and emotional balance in the body. It regulates metabolism and mineral levels, secretes the growth hormone thyrozine, and can stimulate your sex drive. This small, butterfly-shaped gland weighs less than one ounce, yet has an effect on energy level, emotional balance, and the proper functioning of all the other organs.

The thyroid gland controls the rate at which the body generates energy from nutrients. In order to produce a proper amount of hormones for this conversion process, the body requires enough of the mineral iodine. Iodine, which is found in seafood, asparagus, carrots, spinach, and numerous other vegetables, is used to manufacture the thyroid hormone, the principal agent that the thyroid uses to regulate the body's metabolism. If the rate of production is excessively low, a slowing of bodily functions may result and you can develop hypothyroidism. Hypothyroidism may be accompanied by elevated cholesterol, fatigue, emotional sensitivity, and weight gain. It is treated by replacing the normal thyroid hormone with a synthetic hormone that is taken orally. When the thyroid gland begins to run out of control and releases too much thyroid hormone, you run the risk of developing the opposite of hypothyroidism—hyperthyroidism. Symptoms of hyperthyroidism include nervousness, weight loss, rapid heartbeat, bulging of the eyes, perspiration, and even emotional disturbances. Left untreated, hyperthyroidism can result in damage to the heart.

There are four small parathyroid glands located on either side of the thyroid gland. These glands control the level of calcium, minerals, and phosphorous in the blood and bones. Calcium is essential, not only for healthy bones and teeth, but for many other functions including nerve relays, muscle contractions, blood clotting, and gland secretions. A lack of calcium can cause the body to seize calcium from the bones, which leads to fragile bones and possibly osteoporosis. A lack of calcium can also cause twitching, spasms, and convulsions. Too much calcium, on the other hand, may cause a weakening of muscle tone and kidney stones.

How can reflexology help?

Stimulating the thyroid reflex area can help regulate you metabolism and balance your energy. If you know you have a problem with your thyroid, working this area on your feet can be tremendously beneficial in helping the thyroid control hormone production and regain your body's metabolic equilibrium. It can also help relieve PMS!

The thyroid gland reflex point is associated with the fifth chakra, the Throat chakra, which corresponds to communication and innovation. Stimulating this chakra can improve your ability to express yourself to others.

Chakra Association: Fifth chakra, the Throat chakra

Color Association: Blue

Element: Earth

Related Problems: Depression, hypoglycemia, insomnia, menopause, multiple sclerosis,
PMS, psoriasis, low sex drive, impotency, ulcers, thyroid problems
(hypothyroidism/hyperthyroidism)

URETERS (URINARY TRACT)

The reflex area to the urinary tract is located on both feet, in the area between the waist line and the pelvic line, in a narrow strip connecting the kidneys and the bladder. (Although the ureters are not marked on the Reflexology Sox™, you can find them by following the passageway that connects the bladder and kidneys.)

What is it?

The urinary tract consists of a structure that includes the kidneys, two ureters, and the urethra, a tube leading from the bladder to the exterior of the body. It is somewhat like a plumbing system with special pipes that allow water and salts to flow through them. The ureters are tubes leading from the kidneys to the bladder, with muscular walls that contract to make waves of movement that force urine into the bladder.

How can reflexology help?

Stimulating the reflex area to the ureters and the entire urinary tract helps clear any energy blocks and encourage proper elimination of toxins from the body. This can help prevent and relieve urinary tract infections, which are quite common, but it can also boost your energy and strengthen your immune system.

The ureters and the urinary tract reflex points are associated with the second chakra, the Lower Abdomen chakra, which is the center of sexual energy, creativity, and pure emotion. This is the chakra where male sexual energy unites with the female sexual energy, promoting balanced relationships. Stimulating this chakra can enhance your sexuality and boost your libido.

Chakra Association: Second chakra, the Lower Abdomen chakra

Color Association: Orange

Element: Water

Related Problems: Bladder problems, urinary tract infections (UTIs)

PART III:
ORGANS NOT FOUND ON THE REFLEXOLOGY SOX™

ADRENAL GLANDS

The reflex area to the adrenal glands is located on both feet, between the waist line and the diaphragm line. The adrenal glands lie on top of the reflex area to the kidneys and can be worked simultaneously with the kidneys. (Although the adrenal glands do not appear on the Reflexology Sox™, you can find them by locating the reflex areas to the kidneys.)

What are they?

The adrenal glands are actually a two-part endocrine gland that secretes hormones directly into the bloodstream. They are shaped like a three-cornered hat and each gland is perched on each of the kidneys. The glands are about one to two inches in length and weigh only a fraction of an ounce, yet each gland secretes more than three dozen hormones. The adrenals receive information from the pituitary glands, and they affect your physical characteristics, development, and growth level.

Each gland can be divided into two distinct organs. The outer *cortex* region, the yellow-colored layer, secretes hormones which have important effects on the way in which food is used and energy is stored, on substances in the blood, and on physical characteristics such as the shape of your body and the amount of hair you have. The cortex secretes three main types of hormones, called steroids, which control sodium and potassium, help raise blood sugar levels, and affect sexuality.

The smaller, inner *medulla* region of the adrenal gland is the reddish brown layer. Part of the sympathetic nervous system, it is the body's first form of protection and response to physical and emotional stresses. This layer receives instructions from the nervous system and produces chemicals that react to fear, anger, anxiety, and stress. It produces two types of hormones, adrenaline and noradrenaline, which are sometimes called "fight or flight" hormones. These are the hormones you might feel racing through your body just before you're about to do something like bungee jump off a bridge or snow ski down a double black diamond ski run.

How can reflexology help?

Stimulating the reflex areas to the adrenal glands can promote healthy production of the hormones that affect the nervous system, which are often negatively influenced by stress. This helps all of your systems function properly and strengthens your immune system.

The adrenal gland reflex points are associated with the third chakra, the Solar Plexus chakra, which is your energy center for balancing the material and spiritual. Stimulating this chakra can improve your sense of self in the world and can enhance your sense of spirituality.

Chakra Association: Third chakra, the Solar Plexus chakra

Color Association: Yellow

Element: Earth

Related Problems: Arthritis, asthma, autoimmunity disorders, chronic fatigue syndrome, depression, hemorrhoids, high blood pressure, hypoglycemia, impotency, inflammation, multiple sclerosis, low sex drive, prostate problems

APPENDIX

The reflex area to the appendix is located on the right foot, in the same place as the ileocecal valve, which is about two finger-widths below the waist line, below and between the third and fourth toes.

What is it?

The appendix is a worm-like tube, about three to four inches long, which is located between the small intestine and the cecum. It lubricates the large intestine and secretes antibodies into the bloodstream. In some animals, the appendix performs a vital role in digestion and immunity. However, its function in humans is not completely understood except that it does not play any role in the human digestive process. In fact, for a while it was a standard procedure to remove the appendix during any abdominal surgical procedure, just in case it should become a problem in the future. Today, it is recognized that the lymphatic follicles that line the appendix may help to produce some types of immunoglobulins, so the appendix is only removed when it presents significant danger.

Appendicitis is something everyone fears when hit with a painful stomachache. This disorder is an inflammation of the appendix, often due to infection, but sometimes caused by an obstruction of the opening, a tumor, a foreign body, or simply by a kink in the appendix. Appendicitis can cause extreme pain, nausea, and an aversion to food. In a worst-case scenario, it can lead to a rupture of the appendix, which is quite dangerous, as bacteria leaks out of the infected appendix and into the rest of the body. In cases in which appendicitis has been identified, the appendix is usually removed.

How can reflexology help?

Stimulating the reflex area to the appendix can help maintain the health of the large intestine and promote the secretion of antibodies. By stimulating this chakra you can improve creativity and enhance your sexuality.

Chakra Association: Second chakra, the Lower Abdomen chakra

Color Association: Orange

Element: Earth

Related Problems: Appendicitis, gastrointestinal problems

DUODENUM

The reflex area to the duodenum is located on both feet, below the pancreas, from the waist line extending about one inch toward the second toe.

What is it?

The duodenum is the first, C-shaped portion of the small intestine, which is about eight to ten inches long. It's the most fixed portion of the small intestine, and it releases secretions that help the body digest food.

How can reflexology help?

Stimulating the reflex area to the duodenum can strengthen the digestive system, improve food processing, and help the body absorb nutrients and minerals. By balancing this chakra you can also improve your creativity and enhance your sexuality.

> Chakra Association: Second chakra, the Lower Abdomen chakra
>
> Color Association: Orange
>
> Element: Fire
>
> Related Problems: Digestion problems

GALLBLADDER

The reflex area to the gallbladder is located on the right foot only, embedded within the reflex area to the liver, beneath and between the third and fourth toes. It's located about two finger-widths above the waist line.

What is it?

The gallbladder is a small, pear-shaped sac that is situated just below the liver and is attached to it by tissues. The gallbladder is an active storage area that has a capacity of around $1\frac{1}{2}$ fluid ounces. Its role is to help the digestion of food by absorbing mineral salts and water received from the liver, and converting it into a thick, mucus substance called bile, which is released when food is present in the stomach.

How can reflexology help?

Stimulating the reflex area to the gallbladder can help your body digest foods and prevent problems such as heartburn and indigestion. Balancing this chakra can strengthen your sense of power and purpose in the world.

> Chakra Association: Third chakra, the Solar Plexus chakra
>
> Color Association: Yellow
>
> Element: Wood
>
> Related Problems: Digestion problems, gastrointestinal problems

HYPOTHALAMUS

The reflex area to the hypothalamus is the same as the reflex to the pineal gland, which is located on both feet, along the top of the inner edge of the big toe. This area can be stimulated at the same time you work the reflex area to the brain. (Although the pineal gland does not appear on the Reflexology Sox™, you can find it by locating the reflex areas to the brain.)

What is it?

The hypothalamus is a part of the brain that regulates the autonomic nervous system and controls many functions of the body, including emotional responses, hunger, thirst, body temperature, and sleep.

How can reflexology help?

Stimulating this reflex area can soothe your body, regulate your appetite, and improve disrupted sleep patterns. By balancing the energy in this chakra, you encourage a connection with the universe and God or your Higher Power.

> Chakra Association: Seventh chakra, the Crown chakra
>
> Color Association: Purple
>
> Element: Water
>
> Related Problems: Anxiety, eating and sleeping disorders

ILEOCECAL VALVE

The reflex area to the ileocecal valve is located on the right foot, about two finger-widths below the waist line, below and between the third and fourth toes.

What is it?

The ileocecal valve, situated between the small and large intestines, controls the passage of waste in the small intestine through to the large intestine. It also prevents backflow of fecal matter from the large intestine and controls mucous secretions.

How can reflexology help?

Stimulating the reflex area to the ileocecal valve can encourage healthy elimination of waste from the body. Balancing this chakra encourages creativity and enhances your sexuality.

> Chakra Association: Between the second and third chakras, the
> Lower Abdomen chakra/Solar Plexus chakra
>
> Color Association: Orange/Yellow
>
> Element: Fire
>
> Related Problems: Gastrointestinal problems

LYMPH SYSTEM

Lymph vessels are located in many areas of the body, including in the neck, armpits, breasts, abdomen, groin, pelvis, and behind the knees. On the feet, you can find the reflex areas in several places. For lymph drainage in the neck and chest region of the body, the reflex area is located on the front of both feet, in the webbing between the toes. For lymph drainage for the groin and pelvis areas, the reflex area is located across the top of both feet, from the inner anklebone to the outer anklebone, along the same pathway as the reflex area to the vas deferens/fallopian tubes.

What is it?

The lymph system is a network of vessels that filter out foreign particles to prevent infection from passing into the bloodstream. Lymph nodes filter lymph fluid and add lymphocytes, which help defend the body against microorganisms and harmful foreign particles before it is returned to the blood stream. The lymph system also helps to process and eliminate extra protein from tissues.

How can reflexology help?

Stimulating the reflex area to any of the lymph areas can strengthen the immune system and defend against viruses and infections. It helps the body process and eliminate toxins, which decreases fatigue. Balancing the Root chakra allows you to feel more connected and grounded to the earth.

Chakra Association: First chakra, the Root chakra

Color Association: Red

Element: Fire

Related Problems: Hodgkin's disease, immunity problems

PANCREAS

The reflex area to the pancreas is located on both feet, but more on the left foot, below the stomach and above the waist line. On the right foot, it extends to the base of the big toe, and on the left foot it extends to the fourth toe.

What is it?

The pancreas is a long, tapered gland, which lies across from and behind the stomach, and secretes hormones, insulin, and glucagons to regulate the level of glucose in the blood. The pancreas also secretes digestive juices that break down fats, carbohydrates, proteins, and acids, and neutralizes stomach acid. The hormone insulin regulates the use of glucose into all the body tissues except the brain. If the pancreas fails to produce insulin or secretes it in low quantities, the result is a serious disease, diabetes.

How can reflexology help?

Stimulating the reflex area to the pancreas can help regulate blood sugar and prevent problems such as hypoglycemia, hyperglycemia, and diabetes. Balancing the solar plexus chakra can enhance your sense of personal power.

Chakra Association: Third chakra, the Solar Plexus chakra

Color Association: Yellow

Element: Earth

Related Problems: Diabetes, hypoglycemia/hyperglycemia, pancreatic cancer, pancreatitis

PINEAL GLAND

The reflex area to the pineal gland is located on both feet, along the top of the inner edge of the big toe. This area can be stimulated at the same time you work the reflex area to the brain.

(Although the pineal gland does not appear on the Reflexology Sox™, you can find it by locating the reflex areas to the brain.)

What is it?

The pineal gland is a small gland that belongs to the endocrine system and is one of the least understood glands in the body. It is located near the center of the brain in the hypothalamus. The pineal is responsible for producing melatonin, the body's natural hormone for regulating sleep. It responds to daylight and has an effect on our sleeping and waking patterns. For example, if you aren't getting enough daylight, your body may produce too much melatonin and you may have difficulty getting out of bed in the morning. Since sunlight stimulates the pineal to suppress the production of melatonin, you may want to spend more time outside in the sun. Or you may want to open the blinds in the morning and let the sunshine in to wake you up.

The pineal gland also regulates the development of the other glands and helps to maintain a well-balanced and efficient endocrine system. It is thought to contribute to mood and circadian rhythms.

How can reflexology help?

Stimulating the reflex area to the pineal gland can balance mood swings and improve sleep patterns. It has a harmonizing effect on the entire endocrine system that boosts your energy and vitality. Balancing the Third Eye chakra opens your intuitive abilities and helps you to see all things clearly.

Chakra Association: Sixth Chakra, the Third Eye chakra

Color Association: Purple

Element: Water

Related Problems: Depression, insomnia, SAD (seasonal affective disorder, see depression, page 106), PMS

PITUITARY GLAND

The reflex area to the pituitary gland is located on both feet, at the base of the inner edge of the big toe, just below the pineal gland. (Although the pituitary gland does not appear on the Reflexology Sox™, you can find it by locating the reflex area to the brain.)

What is it?

The pituitary gland, which is located in the center of the skull and just behind the bridge of the nose, is one of the most important glands of the body. About the size of a pea, the pituitary gland is an important link between the nervous system and the endocrine system. It controls the functions of all the endocrine glands and releases many hormones that affect growth, sexual development, metabolism, the reproductive system, the mineral and sugar content of the blood, fluid retention, and can also affect the body's energy levels. The pituitary gland helps to keep the body in harmony.

How can reflexology help?

Stimulating the reflex to the pituitary gland can help you maintain healthy metabolism and boost your energy. If you are trying to lose weight, paying extra attention to this area can help your body shed those unwanted pounds. Since this gland is responsible for proper growth of the body's organs and glands, it can be beneficial in stabilizing the growth rate in children, who may be growing too fast or too slowly. Balancing this chakra can strengthen your intuition, perception, and psychic abilities.

Chakra Association: Sixth Chakra, the Third Eye chakra

Color Association: Purple

Element: Water

Related Problems: Chronic fatigue syndrome, depression, hypoglycemia, immunity problems, impotency, insomnia, low sex drive, migraines, sinus problems, weight problems.

SEX ORGANS

For Men: Prostate gland, testes, vas deferens   For Women: Uterus, ovaries, fallopian tubes

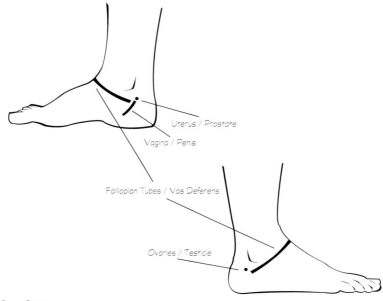

Prostate Gland/Uterus:

The reflex area to the prostate gland and the uterus is located on the inside of both ankles, in the indentation below the anklebone. To locate the area on the inside of the ankle, with the same hand and foot, place your index finger on your heel and your fourth finger on the anklebone. Your middle finger should fall directly on the reflex to the prostate gland in men or the uterus in women.

Testes/Ovaries:

The reflex area to the testes and ovaries is located on the outside of both ankles, in the indentation below the anklebone. To locate the area on the outside of the ankle, place your index finger on the anklebone and your fourth finger on the heel. Your middle finger should fall directly on the reflex to the testes in men or the ovaries in women.

Vas Deferens/Fallopian Tubes:

The reflex area to the vas deferens and fallopian tubes is located in a band across the top of the foot from one ankle bone to the other, linking the reflex areas of the prostate gland and testes in men, and the uterus and ovaries in women.

What is it?

Men:

The male reproductive system consists of sexual organs that are partly visible and partly hidden within the body. The visible parts are the *penis* and the *scrotum*. Inside the body are the *prostate gland* and *vas deferens*, which link the system together. On the outside are the *testes*, a pair of oval-shaped glands suspended in the scrotum, which produce sperm and other male sex hormones. These organs make it possible for a man to produce sperm and fertilize a woman's ova, or eggs.

Prostate gland: The prostate gland is a solid, chestnut-shaped organ surrounding the first part of the urethra in men. Located just under the bladder and in front of the rectum, the prostate gland consists of two main parts that produce the components of semen. The inner part produces a fluid to keep the lining of the male urethra moist, and the outer part produces seminal fluids to assist the passage of semen.

Testes: The testes are the male reproductive glands. They are held inside the scrotum, which is a sac that hangs under the penis. The scrotum is divided internally into two halves by a membrane, and each half contains a testicle. Each testicle produces as many as twelve trillion sperm in a male's lifetime, about 400 million of which are ejaculated during intercourse. Each sperm takes about seventy-two days to mature and its maturity is controlled by a complex interaction of hormones. The scrotum contains a built-in thermostat that keeps the sperm at the proper temperature. The testicles lie in such a vulnerable place, outside the body, because it is too hot inside the body for sperm to be produced and survive.

Vas deferens: The vas deferens are a pair of sperms ducts that are designed to carry sperm from the testes to the urethra. They connect the prostate gland and the two testicles.

Women:

The female reproductive system consists of internal sex glands called *ovaries*, a *uterus*, and *fallopian tubes*.

Uterus: The uterus or "womb" is a hollow, muscular, pear-shaped organ where a fertilized egg, called the *zygote*, is implanted, nourished, and develops until birth. Located in the pelvic cavity behind the bladder and in front of the bowel, the uterus is about four inches long and lined with tissues that change during the menstrual cycle. These tissues grow as a result of hormones released by the ovaries. After a menstrual cycle, the hormones decrease, the blood supply is cut off, and the tissues and unfertilized egg are shed as waste, a "period."

During pregnancy, the uterus stretches from three to four inches in length to the size necessary to accommodate a growing baby. Throughout the nine-month gestation period, the muscular walls of the uterus increase from two to three ounces to about two pounds. These powerful muscles push the baby through the birth canal and then, after the birth, the uterus shrinks back to half its pregnant weight before a baby is a week old. By the time the baby is a month old, the uterus may already be back to the size it was before the pregnancy!

Ovaries: The ovaries are a pair of almond-shaped glands that lie on either side of the uterus and just below the opening to the fallopian tubes. The ovaries are responsible for producing the female sex hormones, called estrogen and progesterone, and storing female sex cells or eggs. A baby girl is born with about 60,000 of these cells, which are contained in sac-like depressions in the ovaries. While each of these cells may have the potential to mature for fertilization, in reality only about 400 ripen during the woman's lifetime.

Fallopian tubes: The fallopian tubes are funnel-shaped tubes, about four to five inches in length, that lie in the pelvic portion of the abdominal cavity and extend from the uterus to the ovaries. Each tube carries eggs and sperm, and is where fertilization of the egg occurs. The larger end of the fallopian tube is divided into feathery, finger-like projections that lie close to the ovary. These projections, along with muscle contractions, force the eggs down the funnel's small end, which opens into the uterus. After sexual intercourse, sperm swim up this funnel from the uterus. The secretions in the lining of the tube can sustain both the egg and the sperm long enough to encourage fertilization and nourish the egg until it reaches its home in the uterus. If an egg splits in two after fertilization, identical or "maternal" twins are produced. If two eggs are fertilized by different sperm, the mother gives birth to non-identical or "fraternal" twins. This all takes place in the fallopian tubes.

How can reflexology help?

Sex is an important part of a normal, healthy lifestyle, and problems in this area can be emotionally and psychologically damaging. For those experiencing problems in the sexual arena, reflexology offers drug-free relief by stimulating the reflex areas that are directly responsible for overall health and the well-being of the body, increasing your sex drive and hormone production, and slowing the aging process. Stimulating the reflex areas to the reproductive organs in both men and women can strengthen libido and improve performance. Balancing the Lower Abdomen chakra can also improve sex drive.

> Chakra Association: Second chakra, the Lower Abdomen chakra
>
> Color Association: Orange
>
> Element: Wood
>
> Related Problems: Depression, impotency, infertility, low sex drive, menopause,
> PMS, prostate problems

HEALING WITH REFLEXOLOGY

Now that you have an idea of how to locate the specific reflex areas on your feet, you're on your way to learning how to heal many of the common problems that can cause discomfort and pain. In the next chapter, you will use the information you learned. Specifically, you'll find the reflexology solutions for many everyday problems. To understand why certain reflex areas should be stimulated to relieve a problem, you may want to refer back to this chapter and refresh your memory about specific body parts. Since many organs have several functions, it's hard to remember everything. To get the most benefit from a reflexology treatment, I suggest that you use this chapter as a point of reference to understand how to treat each problem, through reflexology alone or with a combination of methods that can include color and chakra work.

Chapter 5:
Sole-utions

"I HAVE SAID THAT THE SOUL IS MORE THAN THE BODY,
AND I HAVE SAID THAT THE BODY IS NOT MORE THAN THE SOUL…"

Walt Whitman, "Song of Myself"

One of the best things about reflexology is how easily you can incorporate it into your daily life. Reflexology offers an easy and quick way to get the benefits of a full body massage— and you don't even have to take off your clothes! You can do reflexology almost anywhere, anytime, and you don't need anyone to help you. Use it when you are traveling or in need of quick relief at work. Use it to heal yourself, your family, a friend, a child . . . even a pet.

Reflexology is a drug-free way to effectively relieve many common physical disorders that disturb your well-being (that's why we use the word dis-ease). Sickness and other problems cause imbalances in the body. In this chapter, you'll find many common physical disorders that can damage the health of your body and mind. Following a brief description of each problem and the symptoms that accompany it, you'll find the reflexology solution to help relieve it. To relieve a specific problem, simply follow the instructions for working the reflex area or areas that correspond to that part of the body. Specifically:

1. Look at the chart of the left and right foot, and locate the reflex area to the part of the body you would like to affect.

2. Next, locate that reflex area on your own foot. If you have the Reflexology Sox™ on your feet, it's easy. Simply make sure the toes on each sock are lined up with your toes, and the heel of each sock is lined up with your heel. The Sox™ will stretch to fit any size foot. All of the reflex areas should fall into place so you can find the correct area for different parts of your body on your own two feet.

3. Once you've located "the spot," use any of the techniques detailed in chapter three to affect specific areas of your body.

4. For a more interesting reflexology session, try combining a few techniques.

5. If the reflex area appears on both feet, take the time to work both areas.

6. Remember to pay extra attention to areas that feel "grainy" or tender, as this may indicate that there is a problem with the corresponding part of the body.

7. Spend as much time as you want on each area, but two to three minutes is usually enough. For a "quick fix," simply press your thumb firmly on the area for sixty seconds.

8. As you feel more comfortable with your thumb pressure and the different techniques, your hands will begin to move naturally on the foot. Feel free to experiment and just experience the wonderful sensations on your feet.

Please note that, to avoid repetition, more information on each part of the body, its function, and its associated reflex point is located alphabetically in Chapter Four along with a detailed description of reflex points. Don't be afraid to look there to get a "bigger" picture. When combined with the illustration that follows, labeled by disorder, you will get a very clear idea of just how many solutions lie right beneath you in your feet!

Also realize that the information provided here is general in nature. It should not be used as a substitute for the care and advice of a licensed health care provider. It can, however, be used in conjunction with your physician's medical guidance to help your body's natural healing process along.

ACNE

Reflex areas: Liver, kidneys, bladder, small intestine

Acne can be a teenager's worst nightmare, and is the cause of many painful and awkward memories of adolescence for adults. This common skin disorder is a bacterial infection that affects glands usually found on the face, neck, and upper back. Generally caused by a hormone imbalance, stress, or an overload of toxins in the body, acne affects many adolescents during puberty, pregnant women whose bodies are overrun with hormones, and stressed-out adults. Sometimes, even adults who have never had problems with their skin are afflicted with a breakout of acne. New adult breakouts of acne are often the result of liver congestion, a condition that leads to clogged pores, and eventually pimples.

Reflexology can be used to increase the natural flow of energy throughout the body and help remove some of the toxins that build up in the organs. This in turn serves to control and even prevent acne. Specifically, we use the liver and bladder as detoxifiers, and the kidney point to stimulate the elimination of waste products. Gently work the kidney area, which may be tender, on both feet. Pay attention to little granules that feel like sand by continuing to work on them until they are less tender. These could be signs of kidney stones or other kidney-related problems. Using the finger-walking technique, work your fingers down to the bladder. Finally, work the small intestine so that the body can better absorb nutrients. This also supports toxin expulsion.

ALCOHOLISM/CHEMICAL DEPENDENCY

Reflex areas: Brain, liver, kidney, solar plexus

Alcoholism and other chemical dependencies have serious physical, spiritual, and moral consequences. These dangerous diseases are progressive and chronic, and if left untreated could lead to death. Reflexology can be quite valuable in helping to calm stress and mental anguish in individuals who are fighting the demons of drugs and alcohol. Stimulate the reflex to the brain to relax the mind and strengthen your commitment to maintaining a clean, "chemical-free" body. This can also help soothe headaches that may be caused by withdrawal from drugs or alcohol.

Stimulate the reflex to the liver to detoxify the body and cleanse the body's tissues of any remaining toxins in the system. Too much alcohol is stressful to the liver, so working this area can help the body heal itself. Work the reflex area to the kidneys to promote healthy elimination of water and waste. This also allows the body to detox. Finally, awaken energy in the solar plexus region to calm your nerves and balance all body systems.

ALLERGIES

Reflex areas: Lungs, sinuses, eyes, thymus

Anyone who suffers from allergies can tell you what a horrible feeling it is when your nose is stuffed up, your sinuses are throbbing, your eyes are watering, and you can't stop sneezing. Allergies are caused by the body's immune system overreacting to specific foods, pollens, and other elements. Allergies not only make you sneeze and sniffle, they drain your energy and leave you feeling fatigued for weeks. For those who are prone to allergies, the long-term stress can damage the immune system and make them even more susceptible to allergy attacks. It can even lead to the development of asthma, a condition that afflicts many people, especially children.

While there are currently some very effective drugs on the market, reflexology is an all-natural alternative to medications that may dehydrate your body and make you drowsy. To bring some allergy relief, focus on the reflex areas to the lungs, sinuses, eyes, and thymus. Stimulate the lung area on both feet to strengthen the respiratory system and improve breathing that is weakened by allergies. Working the sinuses, located on the tips of each toe, clears congestion. Massaging the eye reflex point eases itching and watering, while working the thymus boosts your overall immune system, neatly improving sluggish energy levels that accompany allergy attacks.

ANEMIA

Reflex areas: Spleen, liver, heart, lungs

Over 3.3 million women suffer from anemia, a condition characterized by an abnormal decrease in the body's total red blood mass, or hemoglobin. In addition to chronic fatigue and low energy, anemia can cause you to feel sensitive to colder temperatures, have shortness of breath, and can lead to pale lips and cheeks. Many people who just feel tired all the time do not even know that they have anemia until they have a blood test that determines that their iron levels have dipped.

Most people understand anemia as a deficiency of iron in the blood, and it is a serious problem because it can go undetected for a long time. So make sure you eat iron-rich foods such as spinach (think of Popeye), liver, lean meats, salmon, many breakfast cereals, tofu, soybeans, dried beans, oatmeal, seeds such as pumpkin and sesame, and enriched grain products, such as breads, rice, and pasta. You can also help relieve anemia with reflexology by stimulating the reflex areas to the spleen, liver, heart, and lungs.

The spleen point opens up channels that improve the body's ability to filter damaged blood cells. The liver point is also a detoxifier that helps the body process nutrients from your blood, which in turn improves ongoing iron absorption. By working the reflex to the heart you can improve the circulation of blood in the body and diminish the effects of anemia. Lastly, by working the area for the lungs, you encourage a healthy respiratory system and improve the circulation of oxygen through the blood.

ANXIETY

Reflex areas: Solar plexus, stomach, brain

In this day and age, who isn't anxious once in a while? It's a chaotic world, and it is often hard to let go of the day's problems and really relax. Unfortunately this is very damaging to our entire system. Most doctors agree that over seventy-five percent of our health problems today can be linked to stress and tension. When we fail to manage stress, our body's defense mechanism begins to break down, making us more susceptible to illness and disease. Physicians often point to anxiety and stress as the main source of many sexual problems, as well a whole slew of associated discomforts (like headaches, high blood pressure, depression, and ulcers).

In addition to deep breathing and turning to meditation as a way of relieving anxiety, reflexology is extremely effective for calming and balancing the nervous system. It can help you let go of tension and soothe your mind. Reflexology is a drug-free coping mechanism for stress and a way to get in touch with what's happening on the inside. If you have the time, a thirty-minute session covering the entire left and right foot works wonders and can help you forget your worries for a while. If you only have a few minutes, stimulate the reflex areas to the solar plexus, stomach, and brain to quickly bring soothing stress relief.

Press the solar plexus point for twenty to thirty seconds to balance your nervous system and begin the process of reestablishing inner calm. Repeat this several times on each foot. Work the stomach reflex area if you've experienced indigestion or a nervous stomach as a result of other tensions in your life.

The brain reflex point is particularly helpful for workaholics, those who suffer from anxiety attacks, and other people who find it difficult to quiet their minds, which often causes sleep disorders too. Focusing on this point clears away a lot of unnecessary brain chatter. Better still, it makes you more alert, helps relieve stress headaches, and restores a sense of overall harmony.

ARTHRITIS

Reflex areas: Kidneys, liver, adrenal glands

Arthritis, one of the most painful and debilitating diseases that affects people of all ages, especially the elderly, is an inflammation of the joint that typically results in swelling, stiffness, tenderness, pain, and loss of mobility. These joint symptoms may also be accompanied by weight loss, fever, or weakness. Painful symptoms are caused by advanced wear and tear of the protective cartilage. As cartilage deteriorates, the bones rub against each other and can become disfigured or waste away. People who suffer from arthritis may experience so much discomfort that even the most simple tasks, such as tying shoelaces or writing a letter, are extremely difficult to perform.

There are various types of arthritis; some are caused by infection, others by trauma to the body. In many cases, arthritis attacks the linings of the joints, which become painful and swollen. This leads to inflammation of the tissues around the joints and degeneration of the muscles that move the infected joints. *Osteoarthritis* is a common form of degenerative arthritis that affects the weight-bearing joints by attacking the cartilage around the bones. It affects people who are overweight, have a poor blood supply, or who have been injured. *Rheumatoid arthritis*, a progressively debilitating disease that mainly affects the elderly and is more common among women than men, is a chronic viral infection that causes painful inflammation and is often aggravated by stress.

Reflexology can help relieve the pain of arthritis by relaxing the muscles and stimulating the lymphatic system. This helps cleanse the body of toxins and reduces swelling. A reflexology session that covers the entire foot also relieves the stress that aggravates arthritis. A quick solution, however, is to focus on the reflex areas to the kidneys, liver, and adrenal glands.

The kidney point will help in eliminating water retention in the joints. The liver point expels toxins that may contribute to the inflammation of the joints. Additionally, many of the drugs prescribed for rheumatoid arthritis have a toxic nature. So, working this reflex area regularly can be very helpful for people taking those medications. Last, but certainly not least, the adrenal gland point provides pain relief. Pressing firmly on the adrenals' reflex area for a few minutes can release cortisone and the body can begin to heal itself.

ASTHMA

Reflex areas: Lungs, solar plexus, thymus, adrenals

Asthma is one of the most frightening diseases, especially for children, because when you can't breathe your entire body goes into distress. The panic and fear that set in when you suffer from a lack of oxygen in the lungs can cause every muscle in the body to tense up. This places extra stress on all body systems.

Asthma attacks are sporadic and involve wheezing, coughing, and difficulty breathing, especially exhaling. While asthma may be brought about by external factors, such as allergens in the air, it is also directly related to internal factors, such as emotional stress. Unfortunately, many asthma sufferers not only die from lack of oxygen, but also from the drugs that are given for its relief.

Reflexology can help acute and chronic asthma sufferers by relaxing the lungs and transmitting healing energy to the congested area. During allergy season, when asthma attacks often occur, stimulating the reflex areas to the lungs, solar plexus, thymus, and adrenal glands on a daily basis can help to relax the body and may even prevent an asthma attack from beginning. These are also great areas to work when you're sitting on a plane, which often has poor air circulation, or in an area where ventilation is poor. During an asthma attack, time is of the essence and you should not waste precious moments trying to locate and stimulate the reflex points. Instead, use these important reflex areas to relieve anxiety after an attack, and to prevent future asthma attacks.

Stimulate the reflex areas to the lungs on both feet to improve the respiratory system and encourage healthy circulation of oxygen through the blood. Work the solar plexus area for ten seconds then release it several times to restore calm. An easy and effective technique I have taught many clients with chronic asthma is to place both thumbs in the center of the foot, on the solar plexus reflex area. With the rest of the fingers pressing on the top of the foot, gently arch the foot over the thumbs. Release the fingers and flex the foot backwards. Repeat this several times. This movement allows the thumbs to sink deep into the solar plexus reflex, bringing calm and encouraging peace.

We focus on the thymus in order to help to build up the body's natural defenses against external allergens that can cause asthma attacks. Finally, the adrenal gland point controls the "fight or flight" instinct that accompanies an asthma attack as a person struggles for air. For people with chronic and acute asthma, stimulating this area can help to lessen the frequency and severity of asthma attacks.

AUTOIMMUNITY DISORDERS

(see also Multiple sclerosis)

Reflex areas: Thymus, adrenals, solar plexus

Autoimmune disorders occur when the immune system mistakenly attacks the body's own tissues. This reaction, which leads to many diseases that have mild to severe symptoms, may be set off by a number of factors, including infection, tissue damage, or emotional trauma in people who are genetically predisposed to them. While autoimmune diseases are not infectious or contagious, they are serious, debilitating, life-threatening illnesses that affect one in five Americans. There are over eighty known autoimmune diseases, and the most common include rheumatoid arthritis (see Arthritis section, page 98), rheumatic fever, lupus, ulcerative colitis, multiple scle-rosis, thyroiditis, and scleroderma.

Unfortunately, conventional medicine has not found a way to heal these diseases. Therefore, the treatments to manage the debilitating symptoms of autoimmune diseases are suppressive rather than curative. Reflexology helps by opening up channels of energy that help the body heal itself. Work on the reflex areas to the thymus, adrenals, and solar plexus to help get rid of damaging, aggravating stress.

The thymus region is responsible for building up the body's natural defenses. The adrenal gland improves hormone production (those affecting the nervous system) and regulates the body's overall tension levels. The solar plexus area restores a sense of overall harmony, which acts like a tonic on all the body's functions.

BACK PAIN

Reflex areas: Spine, neck, shoulders, brain

"My back is killing me!" Back pain is one of the most common complaints of people all over the world. It affects about seventy-five percent of the population at some time during their adult lives, so chances are you will already have experienced, or are likely to experience, back pain severe enough to make you reduce or even stop normal activity for a while. Most people don't realize the importance of the spine in the well-being of their entire body until something hap-pens and they feel a pinch between their shoulders or a spasm in their lower back. Most back pain is caused from strain in the muscles that support the spine. However, pain in the back is not just a physical problem. It is also a manifestation of anxiety and pressure. Emotional distress often surfaces in the body as chronic back pain. More specifically, emotional stress from rela-tionships often manifests as pain in the middle back, which is directly opposite the Heart chakra.

Sudden, severe pain in the back, often the lower back, is one of the most common, painful, and disabling conditions human beings can suffer. It can occur as a result of lifting a heavy object, tripping or falling, or can be due to viral illness or emotional trauma. The pain may be felt immediately or may develop slowly, getting worse and worse each day. For the most part, the majority of acute back pain is caused by intense muscle spasms. As any woman who has gone through labor will tell you, spasms of the back muscles can be extremely painful and often unbearable. When back spasms, which are caused by a nervous reflex in the spinal cord, are so strong and persistent that they lead to inflammation, a vicious cycle is created that causes even more spasms and inflammation. Worse still, chronic back pain can lead to other problems, including neck and shoulder pain and migraine headaches.

The good news is that reflexology can provide relief, sometimes instantly, from acute and chronic back pain. I have worked with many clients who complained about back pain for years. After just a few reflexology sessions, they could not believe the improvement and relief they felt. Most people who complain of back pain find that the inner soles of their feet are extremely sen-sitive and tender to the touch. I recommend getting a tennis ball and rolling the arch of both feet on it, from the heel of the foot all the way to the toes and back. The pressure of the tennis ball affects the reflex area to the spine just as well as your fingers can affect it. By leaning some of your body weight onto the ball with your foot on top, you can control the pressure and allow the ball to sink in deeply. I find this to be a very relaxing yet invigorating way to start the day.

For the spine point, work your thumbs up and down the inner soles of your feet, concentrating on the area of your back that needs it the most. For lower back pain, spend more time on the area along the inner sole between the heel and the waist line. For middle back pain, work your thumbs along the middle section of the inner edge. For upper back problems, including neck pain, work the area along the inner edge of the foot from the diaphragm line to the base of the big toe. To stimulate the entire back, begin at the heel and thumb-walk up the inner edge of the foot all the way to the base of the big toe. Do this several times, spending extra time on any area that feels tender or "grainy."

Next, work on the neck region to relieve pressure and discomfort. This will also help your entire back, since seven of the spine's thirty-three vertebrae are located here! Similarly, work the shoulder area to alleviate the discomfort in that region and de-stress the entire upper body. Giving some time to the brain area improves nerve/muscle interactions.

Bladder infections (interstitial cystitis)

(See also Urinary tract infections)

Reflex areas: Bladder, kidneys, ureters

Bladder problems are a common and annoying disorder for many people. Running to the bathroom every fifteen minutes, pain while peeing, and an aching back are quite distressing problems. Women, whose urinary anatomy system is more vulnerable to infection than men's, are more susceptible to this problem. Interstitial cystitis, which differs from ordinary cystitis (see Urinary tract infection, page 129), is a chronic inflammation of the bladder, involving scar tissue, stiffening, bleeding, and sometimes ulcers in the bladder walls. The symptoms of this disorder are similar to that of a urinary tract infection, including pain and burning when urinating, urgency, and increased frequency of urination. However, the main difference is that interstitial cystitis can last much longer than a regular UTI and it can lead to permanent damage of the bladder. Reflexology helps by strengthening the energy pathways to the bladder and encouraging proper elimination of toxins from the body. Stimulating the reflex areas to the bladder, kidneys, and ureters helps protect the bladder from this painful and sometimes embarrassing disorder. How? Well, the bladder point is obvious. The kidneys maintain and improve proper elimination, which decreases the chance of infection, and stimulating the ureters clears any congestion of energy on the path between the bladder and kidney. This protects your entire urinary tract and builds your resistance to infections in that part of the body.

Carpal tunnel syndrome (CTS)

Reflex areas: Brain, lungs, solar plexus

Carpal tunnel syndrome is an ever-increasing disorder that is caused by swelling of the tendons that line the carpal tunnel, which is the area between the two wrist bones. The carpal tunnel receives its name from the eight bones in the wrist, called carpals, which form a tunnel-like structure. This tunnel is filled with tendons that control finger movement and it provides a pathway for the median nerve to reach sensory cells in the hand.

Although there are many reasons for developing this swelling of the tendon, carpal tunnel syndrome can result from repetitive and forceful movements of the wrist during work and leisure activities. Repetitive flexing and extension of the wrist may cause a thickening or swelling of the protective sheaths that surround each of the tendons, pressing on the median nerve, and producing the symptoms associated with carpal tunnel syndrome (CTS).

Painful tingling in one or both hands during the night, frequently painful enough to disturb sleep, is one of the first symptoms of CTS. A feeling of uselessness in the fingers, which are sometimes described as feeling swollen even though little or no swelling is apparent, often occurs. As symptoms increase, tingling may develop during the day, commonly in the thumb, index, and ring fingers. A decreased ability and power to squeeze things may follow. In advanced cases, the muscle at the base of the thumb atrophies, and strength is lost. Many patients with CTS are unable to differentiate hot from cold by touch, and experience an apparent loss of strength in their fingers. They appear clumsy and may have trouble performing simple tasks such as tying their shoes or picking up small objects.

The reflexology relief for CTS begins by stimulating the reflex area to the brain. This relieves the pain that may wake you up at night. Stimulating the reflex area to the lungs can improve circulation of blood and oxygen to your entire body, specifically your hands. Working the reflex area to the solar plexus can relax the entire body and relieve some of the stress in your wrists. Finally, apply pressure with your thumb to the top of the opposite wrist, in the area between the two bones. This directly affects the carpal tunnel.

When I first began working as a massage therapist, I spent many hours using my hands and definitely overworked my muscles. As I began to feel the early symptoms of carpal tunnel syndrome (a painful, throbbing, aching in my hands that actually woke me up at night), I started to stretch my hands regularly and stimulate specific reflex areas in my feet. Luckily, the symptoms disappeared and I am carpal tunnel syndrome-free!

CHRONIC FATIGUE SYNDROME (CFS)

Reflex areas: Adrenals, brain, pituitary, solar plexus

I'll bet that almost everybody knows at least one person who has this disease. Chronic fatigue syndrome (CFS) is a debilitating illness that is characterized by at least six months of unexplained fatigue (feeling extremely tired or exhausted), together with impaired concentration or memory, and variable other physical signs and symptoms. In the United States, it is estimated that CFS currently affects four to ten of every 100,000 Americans over eighteen years of age, with twice as many women afflicted as men. Although CFS can attack people of all age groups, including children, it is most common in people who are twenty-five to forty-five years old.

In many patients with CFS, the disorder begins suddenly, often following a flu-like infection or an episode of physical or emotional trauma. In other cases, CFS develops gradually. Unfortunately, at this time the exact cause of chronic fatigue syndrome remains a mystery. In order to diagnose this disorder, most physicians look for the fatigue to be severe enough to cause a more than fifty percent reduction in usual activities. In addition to continual fatigue, people with CFS exhibit at least four more symptoms that must persist for at least six months. These symptoms include impaired concentration or short-term memory, a sore throat, enlarged lymph nodes (swollen glands) in the neck or underarm area, muscle pain, pain in several joints, headaches, sleep that doesn't refresh, or an extreme reaction to physical exertion that leaves you feeling sick for at least twenty-four hours.

Using reflexology to combat CFS can be quite effective. I have several clients who suffer from CFS and use reflexology regularly as a healing therapy. While the debilitating symptoms of this disease do not typically disappear quickly, they can be suppressed enough so that you may function better. Reflexology is one key to reviving your energy and re-balancing your entire body.

Begin by working the adrenal gland point simultaneously with the kidneys to stimulate a healthier production of hormones. Move to the brain area of both feet next. This improves energy pathways throughout the body, but specifically the energy pathway between the brain and the pituitary and adrenals, the two endocrine glands that may play a role in the development of CFS.

By massaging the pituitary gland, you can positively affect all the endocrine glands and release many hormones that affect growth, sexual development, metabolism, the reproductive system, the mineral and sugar content of the blood, fluid retention, and the body's energy levels. These are all functions that are disturbed and damaged by CFS. Then it's on to the solar plexus to help reclaim the energy often zapped by CFS. Try it on yourself any time you feel run down. People swear it works!

COLDS AND FLU

Reflex areas: Thyroid, thymus, lungs, sinuses, eyes

Got a runny nose, sinus congestion, sneezing, sore throat, cough, and fever? Then you probably have a cold or the flu. Cold and flu viruses attack the nose, nasal sinuses, throat, and the upper breathing tubes (trachea and bronchi). Colds are undoubtedly the most common illness in the world. In the United States, ninety percent of the population suffers through at least one cold per year. The flu is similar, often producing the same symptoms as a cold, but it's often much more severe and lasts longer.

While colds and flu are both caused by viruses, the real difference between them is simply the type of virus that causes them. The only way to catch a cold or flu is from other people. And infected people can spread the virus from a day or two before they even have symptoms to three or four days after the symptoms start! To prevent colds and flu, wash your hands often and stay away from people who are sneezing or coughing. In addition, reflexology can strengthen your body against these viruses and help prevent you from getting sick.

To start this process, work the sinuses to clear congestion. Next, move to the lung point not only to improve breathing, but also to strengthen your respiratory system. If your eyes have been itchy or watery, work that point too. There are other problems that often accompany a cold and flu, like a stiff neck. Don't overlook the associated reflex points when you're trying to give yourself some relief. Working the neck can also deter sore throats.

To boost your overall immune system and help prevent colds and flu, look to the thymus reflex area. Finally, for overall improved energy to fight such illnesses, stimulate the thyroid point.

COLIC

Reflex areas: Stomach, colon, small intestine

According to the American Academy of Pediatrics, approximately one in five infants develops colic, usually between the ages of two and four weeks, and it ends when the infant is between three and five months. Doctors don't know what causes colic, which is characterized by excessive crying, fussiness, sensitivity, and wakefulness that lasts at least three hours a day, three days a week, and continues for three weeks. While most babies cry an average of one to three hours a day, colicky babies cry much longer, often screaming, pulling up their legs, and passing gas.

Colic is difficult to understand because just about anything can cause your baby to cry. While the exact cause of colic remains a mystery, possible causes are immaturity of the gastrointestinal system, immaturity of the central nervous system, and simply the infant's temperament. As the nervous system matures at around three to six months, your baby should calm down. Massaging your baby's belly can significantly reduce the amount of time he or she spends crying. (See Suggested Further Reading, Living Arts Baby Massage video.)

While there is no proven cure for colic, it's important to remember that colic is a condition that a baby just has to grow out of. Reflexology offers a means to soothe your baby which will, in turn, calm your nerves. When you stimulate a baby's foot, try to be extra gentle and use very light pressure. Watch the baby's cues and continue as long as she is comfortable and happy.

In particular, pay attention to the stomach point to get rid of gas and cramps. Also stimulate the colon on both feet, starting with the right foot first, to help move gas and waste matter out of the baby's body. From here you can move to the small intestine point, which also encourages waste elimination. Since babies' gastrointestinal systems may be immature, working this reflex area can send healing energy to the intestines, which strengthens and supports the entire system.

COLON PROBLEMS

Reflex areas: Colon, small intestine, stomach, solar plexus

Diverticulosis/diverticulitis

Diverticulosis and diverticulitis are two common conditions that affect the colon. Diverticulosis is the development of small, abnormal pouches in the wall of the colon. Diverticulitis is the inflammation of these pouches, which often leads to episodes of cramping, lower abdominal pain, and constipation, or even worse, constipation alternating with diarrhea. While diverticulosis is usually symptomless, stress and poor diet can advance the development of the more distressing diverticulitis. If diverticulitis is complicated by infection, symptoms can include nausea, fever, cramping, and severe pain on the left side of the body. In very extreme cases, diverticulitis can cause intestinal obstruction. Treatment for active infections or serious intestinal obstructions begins with antibiotics, a controlled diet, and sometimes surgery.

Approximately 300,000 cases of diverticulosis are diagnosed every year, and while it is rare in people under forty years of age, fifty percent of all people over the age of sixty have some growth of one or more abnormal pouches. Diverticulosis has been linked to diets high in fat and low in fiber. Unsurprisingly, it is widespread in Western countries, but is notably less common in Asia and Africa, where diets contain less fat and processed food. Often, there are no symptoms at all. People do not know that they even have diverticulosis until an infection develops. If you have either of these conditions, it's helpful to improve your diet and learn techniques to prevent stress from derailing your digestive systems. Consequently, work the reflex areas noted above while changing your diet, then continue reflexology afterward as a maintenance plan.

Irritable bowel syndrome (IBS)

Irritable bowel syndrome (IBS) is a recently recognized condition of the colon that is not very well understood. An estimated fifteen million Americans suffer from this condition, which has also been called spastic or irritable colon, mucus colitis, and functional bowel syndrome, yet only twenty percent seek medical help. In fact, IBS is the second most common cause of work and school absenteeism, and twice as many women than men have IBS.

IBS is a syndrome that involves problems with the lower digestive tract. While symptoms vary and change over time, IBS is characterized by a combination of persistent and recurrent abdominal pain and colon spasms, as well as diarrhea, constipation, or both. People who suffer from IBS have a hypersensitive gastrointestinal tract. Pain recurringly begins after eating and goes away after a bowel movement. However, sometimes the nerves are so sensitive that normal contractions, even with digesting a normal meal, can be extremely painful. I know people who experience such excruciating spasms in their colon that they have to be admitted to the hospital.

While doctors are not exactly sure what causes IBS, it is aggravated by poor diet, anxiety, stress, and other psychological factors. While stress can affect bowel function in anyone, the effect is greater in people with IBS. IBS is considered a functional disorder, and there is no inflammation, infection, or abnormal growths that would show up on these tests. Therefore, it is often hard to diagnose. Fortunately, as individuals get older, symptom intensity may reduce or become less of a problem. Lifestyle changes and learning how to cope with stress are normally recommended for this disorder, and of course, reflexology!

Crohn's disease

Crohn's disease is another painful disorder of the colon that involves inflammation that damages the whole wall of the colon, not just the superficial lining. Crohn's disease involves the small intestine as well as the large intestine, and it is even more resistant to treatment than ulcerative colitis. This disease may affect isolated parts of the intestines, with healthy, normal tissue remaining in between damaged tissue. The symptoms are similar to those of ulcerative colitis, including diarrhea, abdominal pain, weight loss, and mild fever.

Ulcerative colitis

Ulcerative colitis is a painful disease in which the inner layer if the colon becomes inflamed and develops ulcers. In addition to abdominal cramping and pain, it can also cause bloody diarrhea, mild fever, weight loss, and a great many complications that often require drastic treatments. Unlike Crohn's disease, which can affect the entire intestines, ulcerative colitis is limited to the large intestine. While doctors believe that autoimmunity plays a role in this disease, they don't know the exact causes that trigger "episodes," which are sometimes so excruciating that you end up in the hospital and require morphine. Doctors normally treat chronic ulcerative colitis with strong drugs, including long-term steroids. However, if these fail to control the problem, then all or part of the colon is removed.

All of these painful disorders of the colon follow alternating cycles of exacerbation and remission. Therefore, the goal for treating these diseases should be to encourage remission rather than suppress the inflammation after an episode. Since massage of the abdomen area is not recommended for any of these diseases because it could aggravate the intestines, reflexology can help to encourage healing by unblocking congestion on the intestines. It also calms the inflammation and prevents painful future episodes.

For all of these disorders affecting the colon, stimulate the following reflex areas:

- The colon, starting left foot first, beginning at the base of the ascending colon and moving up and across the transverse colon. To work the right foot, begin at the inner edge of the transverse colon and move towards the outer edge and then down the descending colon.
- The small intestine, to encourage proper elimination of waste mater and decrease toxins that can cause symptoms.
- The stomach, to alleviate cramping or bloating (and strengthen digestion).
- The solar plexus, pressing for ten seconds then releasing several times. This balances the nervous system.

DANDRUFF

Reflex areas: Kidneys, thyroid, adrenals, solar plexus

The white, snowy flakes of dandruff on someone's shoulders or hair is not an attractive sight. Everyone's body surface continuously sheds dead skin cells every twenty-four days. Dandruff is a natural process caused by an excessive rate of shedding of dead skin cells from the scalp. This embarrassing problem, which can occur anywhere on the scalp, usually appears as small, round, white-to-gray patches that itch and flake on the top of the head.

Dandruff has a seasonal cycle that's most severe during the winter and mildest during the summer. It can also be caused by excessive use of hairsprays, gels, or electric hair curlers, improper use of hair-coloring products, cold weather and dry indoor heating, tight-fitting hats and scarves, infrequent shampooing, inadequate rinsing, and stress. While you can't completely eliminate dandruff because it's a natural body process, you can control it by regularly shampooing, using medicated anti-dandruff shampoo, and trying reflexology!

To promote proper water elimination that can help deter dandruff, work the kidney areas on both feet. Combine this with the thyroid for chemical and emotional balance, the adrenals to promote healthy hormone production and decrease stress, and the solar plexus to encourage harmony, decrease anxiety, and slow down the overly rapid shedding of skin cells.

DEPRESSION

Reflex areas: Adrenals, brain, pituitary, pineal, heart, thyroid

Depression is a universal characteristic of humankind, and feelings of sadness, anger, and grief are natural reactions to losses or changes in your life. However, what makes these reactions normal is that people eventually recover. It is when sadness never returns to joy that it becomes the nation's leading psychological problem: clinical depression.

There are several different types of depression and it's important to distinguish between situational depression, which is a normal reaction to external events, and endogenous depression, which is unrelated to situations and may be linked to a chemical imbalance in the brain. Some of the most common types are mild depression (dysthymia), major depression, manic depression (bipolar), atypical depression, and post-partum depression. Seasonal affective disorder (SAD), otherwise known as the "winter blues," is a condition that develops due to lack of sunlight. Typically, mild or major depression develops in late fall and clears up in early spring, when the sun reappears. The months of December, January, and February are usually the most unpleasant for people with this disorder.

Depression typically involves sadness, lethargy, and in serious cases, despair, anger, insomnia, loss of appetite or weight gain, obsessive thoughts, and thoughts of suicide. Since the various types of depression are not precisely defined, it's important to seek medical guidance to determine the seriousness of the problem. Treatments can involve psychological counseling as well as anti-depressant medications.

Reflexology can help all of types of depression by stimulating areas of the brain that affect our moods and energy levels. What's more, it can strengthen our body rhythms as well as rebalance the body's chemical and emotional functions. Stimulate the reflex areas to the adrenals, brain, pituitary, pineal, and solar plexus.

The adrenal gland area is especially helpful for a quick boost if you're feeling down and out, with no energy. The brain reflex point improves mental clarity. The pineal gland helps regulate sleeping patterns (often disrupted by depression) and balance the endocrine system.

Next, the pituitary gland point on both feet is a great "pick me up." The heart point clears energy blockages to uplift your spirits and soothe your soul. The solar plexus reflex point is very invigorating and the thyroid point motivates overall equilibrium.

DIGESTION PROBLEMS

(heartburn and indigestion)

Reflex areas: Stomach, neck, solar plexus

Have you ever felt a burning sensation after eating a slice of pizza or a greasy hamburger? If so, you may have experienced heartburn or indigestion. Heartburn, a reflux action doctors refer to as "esophagitis," is a common condition that affects fifty percent of all Americans at least once a month, and seven percent on a daily basis. Twenty-five percent of all pregnant women experience it daily at some point during their pregnancy. Heartburn is characterized by a burning feeling in the middle of your chest that is caused by acid leaking upwards from the stomach into the esophagus, or swallowing tube. It can also cause nighttime coughs, wheezing, and in some cases, difficulty swallowing food due to scarring of the esophagus.

Acid indigestion, almost as common as heartburn, is characterized by a similar burning sensation, but in the pit of your stomach rather than the esophagus. It is caused by acid irritating the stomach lining or duodenum, as well as insufficient protection from the mucus that lines the stomach. Peptic ulcers develop when acid indigestion burns your stomach so much that lesions similar to canker sores develop.

To prevent heartburn, you must tighten the loose esophagus where it meets the stomach to avoid stomach acid from splashing back up. To prevent acid indigestion, you need to protect the stomach lining and avoid activities that increase stomach acid. You can do this by staying upright long enough to allow food and acid to empty out of your stomach, and avoiding certain foods that can irritate your stomach.

Reflexology also helps by calming the stomach and esophagus, and sends healing energy to maintain their protective layers. Stimulate the stomach point to soothe any irritation or burning sensation, work the neck area to relieve the throat pain, and massage the solar plexus to relieve any associated stress that goes along with feeling lousy.

EAR PROBLEMS

Reflex areas: Ears, neck, thymus, solar plexus

Ear infections and tinnitus (also known as ringing in the ears) are the most common problems that affect the ears. Infections are a widespread childhood illness, and two out of three children have at least one episode by their third birthday. Ear infections develop when either bacteria or viruses invade the middle ear, which is located just behind the eardrum, and pus builds up causing pain, pressure, and inflammation. As the eardrum becomes inflamed and stops vibrating normally, there is usually some temporary loss of hearing.

A child's eustachian tube, which is the tube that runs from the inner ear to the back of the throat, is shorter than an adult's is. Therefore, it is easier for bacteria and viruses to find their way to the ear via this short pathway. Sometimes, in severe ear infections, the pressure of the infection may actually cause the eardrum to rupture. Once this happens, the fever usually drops, ear pain suddenly stops, and pus begins to drain into the ear canal. However, if an ear infection itself persists, it can cause permanent damage to the middle ear and eardrum.

Tinnitus, characterized by an annoying buzzing or ringing in the ears, can be caused by excess ear wax (clean those ears!), possible damage to the eardrum, overuse of certain blood-thinning drugs (including aspirin), or a lack of magnesium. This irritating and upsetting problem has no cure. However, reflexology can help.

In the ears, there exist as many reflex points as there are in the feet. This makes the ears particularly responsive to reflexology and to the energy that flows when you stimulate the reflex area on each foot, just below the base of the pinkie and fourth toes. In addition to stimulating this reflex area, you can also work on the ear point itself, the thymus, neck, and solar plexus.

Begin by working the ear reflex area to soothe inflammation and reduce wax build-up. Next, move to the neck to help clear the eustachian tube. Follow with the thymus to boost your overall immune system to help protect against future ear infections, then finally to the solar plexus to sooth the mental irritation that naturally accompanies this kind of painful problem.

EMPHYSEMA

Reflex areas: Lungs, neck, solar plexus

Emphysema is a widespread disease of the lungs, which afflicts 1.8 million Americans in the U.S. alone. Many of the people with emphysema are older men, but the condition is rapidly increasing among women. Smoking is responsible for eighty to ninety percent of emphysema cases. In addition, it is estimated that 50,000 to 100,000 Americans living today were born with a deficiency of a protein that causes an inherited form of emphysema. Emphysema doesn't develop suddenly, but rather comes on gradually; it takes years of exposure to the irritation of cigarette smoke.

It is known from scientific research that the normal lung has a remarkable balance between two classes of chemicals with opposing actions. The elastic fibers in the lung sac allow the lungs to expand and contract. When the chemical balance is altered, the lungs lose the ability to protect themselves against the destruction of these elastic fibers. Eventually, they lose their elasticity and are able to transfer less and less oxygen to the bloodstream, which causes shortness of breath; this is commonly known as emphysema.

Reflexology can help soothe the symptoms of emphysema by clearing the energy to the lungs, and relaxing the neck and throat area. This strengthens the entire respiratory system and eases breathing problems. Stimulating the reflex area to the solar plexus relaxes the diaphragm and calms the nervous system, which may be stressed as the body struggles to inhale and exhale.

I used to work with an eighty-five year old woman who had smoked since she was fifteen. In addition to poor—or almost no—circulation to her extremities, she suffered from such terrible emphysema that she had to be connected to an oxygen tank at all times. When I stimulated the reflex area to her lungs, it seemed as if her whole body relaxed and she would breathe a long sigh of relief. She said that her weekly reflexology treatments were the only time she felt that she didn't have to strain to take a breath.

EYE PROBLEMS

Reflex areas: Eyes, brain, kidneys, thymus

The eyes are the windows to the soul. It's usually not until there is something wrong with them that most people begin to appreciate how significant they are. There are many disorders that affect the eyes, and even the mildest can cause anxiety. Eyestrain, a common complaint among those who spend many hours reading or staring at a computer, can lead to painful headaches in the front of the head. Cataracts and macular degeneration are two common causes of visual impairment in older people. Conjunctivitis, or "pinkeye," is a common inflammation of the delicate membrane that lines the inside of the eyelid and surface of the eye.

I recently had LASIK surgery to correct near-sightedness in both eyes. After sixteen years of wearing contact lenses, I cannot tell you how amazing it was to wake up the day after the surgery and see everything clearly, with almost 20/20 vision. For the weeks following the surgery, I worked the reflex areas to the eyes on both feet. In the beginning, the areas felt a little tender, almost as if they were bruised. For the next two weeks I continued to work this area and the tenderness eventually disappeared. At the same time, my eyes healed perfectly and I had no problems with infections or blurring. While I had a wonderful doctor who was an expert in the field, I firmly believe that reflexology helped me recover quickly, with no complications. Now, I wake up every-day and am so happy to see the clock across the room!

From this experience, I can honestly testify that reflexology can absolutely help to strengthen the eyes and protect them so that you will see the world with clarity. Stimulate the reflex areas to the eyes, brain, kidneys, and thymus. The eye area helps to relieve infections and prevent muscle deterioration. The brain area can deter headaches from eyestrain. The reflex to the kidneys is one of the most important points, since kidneys affect the normal functioning of the eye, and the thymus point boosts your immune system so you won't fall prey to bacteria or viruses than can cause infections.

FATIGUE

(See chronic fatigue syndrome)

FOOT PAIN

Are your feet killing you? If so, you may have a common foot problem caused by your shoes. While reflexology may not get rid of the cause of your problem (since you have to wear shoes), a relaxing foot rub can help minimize your agony. To relieve any of the following problems, stimulate the entire foot, and then follow the suggestions for other soothing sole-utions.

PROBLEM	SYMPTOM	SOOTHING SOLE-UTIONS
Bunions	A bony bump at the base of the big toe	Apply ice. Avoid high heels.
Calluses	Patches of hardened or thickened skin	Soak feet in warm water to soften skin, then use pumice stone to file callus away.
Corns	Red, thick areas of skin on tops or between toes	Follow sole-ution for calluses. Try over-the-counter corn pads.
Hammertoes	Painful, curled, claw-like toes	Wear wide, comfortable shoes. Use over-the-counter pads.
Plantar Fascitis	Arch and/or heel pain that feels like a bruise	This is an inflammation of the ligament of the sole. Apply ice; wear well-cushioned shoes.
Ingrown toenail	Pain and swelling near edge of toenail	Soak feet in warm water. Avoid over-trimming corners, which can cause nails to grow into the skin.
Neuroma	Pain and numbness on the ball of the foot, into the toes	Place a pad in shoes under the ball between the third and fourth toes. Wear wide, soft shoes.

GASTROINTESTINAL PROBLEMS

Constipation

Reflex areas: Colon, small intestine, stomach, brain

Not surprisingly, constipation is the most common gastrointestinal complaint in the United States, resulting in about two million annual visits to the doctor—and millions of dollars in laxative sales! According to the 1991 National Health Interview Survey, about four and a half million people in the United States say they are constipated most or all of the time. The majority of these complaints are from women, children, and adults over the age of sixty-five. During pregnancy, constipation is a common complaint.

At one time or another almost everyone gets constipated. The usual causes are poor diet (lack of fiber), dehydration, lack of exercise, stress, and anxiety. Other factors may be medications, irritable bowel syndrome, travel, changes in your routine, and holding back the urge "to go."

Some people simply have trouble "letting go." In most cases, constipation is temporary and not serious. People who are constipated may find it difficult and painful to have a bowel movement, and suffer from gas, abdominal pain, and headaches. Other symptoms of may include feeling bloated, uncomfortable, and sluggish. While some people believe you should have three bowel movements a day, every body is different. Only you know when your body "isn't right" and you just can't go.

Reflexology (along with increasing your water and fiber intake) can stimulate the peristaltic action of the colon to help you release toxins and waste in your body. When waste stays in your body for long periods of time, your body can become "toxic" and feel fatigued. Healthy elimination is necessary to balance your system and reenergize yourself. Colon hydrotherapy is an alternative to laxatives, which many people overuse and abuse. Remember, happiness is a healthy colon!

Speaking of which, let's move to the colon reflex area. It's best to work the left foot first, beginning at the base of the ascending colon and moving up and across the transverse colon. To work the right foot, begin at the inner edge of the transverse colon and move towards the outer edge and then down the descending colon. Stimulating this reflex area on both feet can begin peristalsis, which is waves of muscular contractions that push waste through the colon. I have actually had people stop their reflexology session while I am working on this area because all of a sudden they are overcome with the urge "to go." Working this reflex area on a regular basis can promote regularity of the bowels and keep your whole body energized.

Next, focus on the small intestine. This eliminates toxins that may slow your body down and make you feel bloated. Also work on the stomach to relieve the bloating and tummy aches you feel as a result of constipation. It encourages the digestive system to move food through the body and eliminate waste quicker. Finally, work the brain reflex point. People who are constipated often have headaches caused by toxins that are literally "stuck" in their system. Stimulating this area can relieve headache pain and can also take your mind off the uncomfortable feeling in your bowels.

Diarrhea

Reflex areas: Stomach, small intestine, colon, kidneys

Ever heard of Montezuma's Revenge? If you've been so unlucky to suffer through it, you certainly know what diarrhea is. The opposite of constipation, diarrhea is the body's general reaction to anything that attacks or irritates the intestines, including intestinal infections, parasites, irritating chemicals, even a new kind of food or medicine. It's one of the most uncomfortable and embarrassing disorders you can have, especially when traveling in a foreign country. Unfortunately, approximately twenty-five to fifty percent of the three million tourists who travel to Mexico each year return with diarrhea. Luckily, in eighty percent of cases the symptoms last less than a week.

Diarrhea results when there is some kind of interference with the large intestine's capacity to absorb liquid from solid wastes that are passed down to the small intestine. Traveler's diarrhea, a feared malady for even the most seasoned travelers, is a bacterial infection caused by unsanitary handling of food. The worst part about this particular infection is that it's passed on via the "fecal-oral" route; in other words, it's mainly caused when food handlers do not wash their hands properly after they use the bathroom and then they touch your food. Now that's something to think about the next time you're in a restaurant!

Reflexology applied to the stomach, small intestine, and colon reflex areas can be helpful in strengthening the digestive system. This relaxes the stomach, rebalances the elimination of fluid and waste, and promotes healthy regularity, which is something we all want.

HAIR

(thinning or baldness)

Reflex areas: Thyroid, pituitary, lungs

Hair loss is probably one of the most alarming problems for men (and some women) as they get older. On average, everybody loses fifty to one hundred and fifty hairs each day, but most hair grows back because the follicle remains intact. Problems arise when hair doesn't grow back. Every hair on your head follows a genetically programmed schedule that includes growth, resting, and shedding. Baldness occurs when shedding significantly exceeds growth. In ninety-five percent of people, a hair loss disorder is genetic. If you are predisposed to hair loss, the first thing you notice is thinning hair. Eventually the hair follicle dies, there is no growth of new hair, and permanent baldness occurs.

In addition to hereditary factors, high levels of stress have been known to cause some hair loss, but this is usually temporary. Autoimmune disease, the use of certain drugs, illness, and severe nutritional deficiency may also cause hair loss or promote early male-pattern baldness. Trauma to the head together with scarring can also cause permanent damage to hair follicles. Even tight hairdos like braids or taut up-dos can create tension that might damage hair follicles, destroying them and stopping hair growth. Since good circulation and healthy blood are essential to our hair, reflexology can help by activating the reflexes to the parts of the body that contribute to hair growth.

Begin by working the thyroid to promote healthy hair follicles and new hair growth. Stimulate this area to awaken hair follicles and prevent hair loss. Next, move to the lung area. Good circulation is essential to healthy hair and working this area enriches the blood with oxygen. Finally, work the heart reflex point to effectively improve the circulation of blood and encourage healthy activity of your body's cells and tissues.

HANGOVERS

Reflex areas: Liver, kidneys, stomach, solar plexus

Had a rough night? One too many drinks? If you wake up with a throbbing head, an upset stomach, tired eyes, and the feeling of a heavy cloud hanging over your head, you are in desperate need of hangover help. Rather than just lying in bed waiting for the alcohol to leave your body and to feel better, be proactive and take control of your hangover. Get up and find those Reflexology Sox™. If you can't see straight, ask someone to press on the area for "hangover help."

Reflexology really can help relieve the after-effects of too much alcohol. While I recommend stimulating the entire foot to soothe your entire body, even just a few minutes spent working these four reflex areas can perk you up. Try it... It works!

Start with your liver point in order to help push out the remaining alcohol in your body. Move to the kidneys, which coordinate with the liver in the elimination process, and drink lots of water! If you're experiencing nausea, massage the stomach point, and the solar plexus region if you find your entire sense of center has been disrupted by the hangover.

Headaches

(See also migraines)

Reflex areas: Brain, eyes, neck, shoulders, back, solar plexus

Feeling like your head is going to explode? Everybody has had a headache at one time or another. They can be caused by many different reasons, but the most common are probably stress and muscle tension. Tension headaches, a very common stress-related disorder, usually develop in the afternoon (after a stressful day) and produce steady pain that comes up the neck and back of the head. This pain can lead to muscle tension that radiates from the neck to the shoulders and down the back. Tension headaches can also be caused by musculo-skeletal problems in the upper back and neck.

If you suffer from sinus pressure or eyestrain, you may experience the type of headache pain that develops in the forehead or around the eyes. Or, if you have high blood pressure, you may experience a headache that develops in the back of the head and surfaces when you wake up. Frequent or persistent headaches can be an indicator that your blood pressure is elevated.

A headache that is throbbing is a "vascular" headache, which arises from an imbalance in the arteries of the head. Vascular headaches are the primary result of caffeine withdrawal as well as a common symptom of caffeine addiction. The most common type of vascular headache is a migraine (See migraine, page 120), yet many people also suffer from cluster headaches, which come about in clusters, at the same time of day, over several days or weeks. Cluster headaches, like migraines, are extremely painful. They are typically one-sided and may cause redness and tearing of the eye on the affected side, runny nose or nasal stuffiness, and visible swelling of blood vessels on the affected side of the head.

Many people turn to drugs for quick relief of headaches. Now you can turn to reflexology to bring relief from the pain more quickly. Stimulate the reflex areas to the brain, eyes, neck, shoulder, back, and solar plexus. The brain point releases congested energy, eases your aching mind, and sends healing energy throughout your entire body. The eye reflex area helps relieve headaches caused by eyestrain. The neck area relieves some pressure and throbbing in that region and can help keep the neck relaxed so the headache doesn't return.

If you find you're wearing your shoulders like earrings when you have a headache, don't overlook this reflex area. It will help de-stress your entire upper body. Working the reflex area to the spine relieves muscle tension and soothes your back, which in turn decreases head pain. And, as with other disorders, if you find that the headache has really disrupted an otherwise good day, work the solar plexus point to restore a sense of calm and wholeness.

Hemorrhoids

Reflex areas: Hemorrhoids, colon, adrenals

Alas, almost everyone is bothered by hemorrhoids at one time or another. About half of the population over the age of fifty has them! Many people, however, have no idea what they are—and have no real desire to learn. If you're interested, hemorrhoids are actually distended veins around the anus that can become inflamed, causing itching, pain, and rectal bleeding.

Similar to varicose veins in the legs, hemorrhoids are swollen blood vessels in and around the anus and lower rectum that stretch under pressure. They can occur either inside the anus (internal) or under the skin around the anus (external). Hemorrhoids can be caused by increased pressure and swelling from straining at the stool, prolonged sitting, genetics, aging, irritants in the diet, and chronic constipation or diarrhea. They are quite common among pregnant women due to the pressure of the fetus in the abdomen and hormonal changes, which cause the blood vessels to enlarge. Fortunately, for most women, hemorrhoids caused by pregnancy are only temporary.

The good news is that hemorrhoids are not usually dangerous or life threatening, and more often than not, the symptoms will disappear within a few days. In fact, many people have hemorrhoids and never experience any symptoms. If you do have symptoms, however, reflexology can help soothe the soreness and irritation.

Begin with the area associated with hemorrhoids (the same as that for the rectum and lower colon). This should help relieve some itching and pain. Working the colon area encourages healthy elimination and prevents hemorrhoids from developing, and working the adrenal gland reflex area produces an anti-inflammatory hormone that can soothe irritated, hemorrhoidal blood vessels.

HERNIA

Reflex areas: Stomach, lungs, neck

A hernia, often referred to as a "window of weakness" that has opened up in the wall tissue of the body, is the protrusion of an organ through the wall of the cavity that contains it. A hiatal hernia is a widespread condition in which a portion of the stomach protrudes upward into the chest and causes chest pain, heartburn, indigestion, difficulty swallowing, and many other symptoms. In some cases, however, there are no symptoms present at all. Hiatal hernias are common, especially in people who are overweight, smoke, or are over the age of fifty.

While the exact cause of a hiatal hernia is not known, it is believed to be the result of a weakening of the support tissue. To reduce the symptoms of a hiatal hernia, doctors suggest that you avoid large or heavy meals, never lie down or bend over immediately after eating, watch your weight, and cut down or stop smoking. In severe cases, physicians may prescribe medications that neutralize the stomach acidity, or that strengthen the lower esophageal sphincter. As a helpmate, reflexology relaxes the stomach and chest, and strengthens the tissues that support them.

Start with the stomach reflex area to reduce pain and distress. Move to the lungs to strengthen the respiratory system and chest cavity. End with the neck to alleviate the painful heartburn and indigestion caused by a hiatal hernia, and to help you swallow better.

HIGH BLOOD PRESSURE (HYPERTENSION)

Reflex areas: Adrenals, brain, solar plexus

High blood pressure is often called the "silent killer," because it usually has no symptoms. In fact, many people have high blood pressure for years without knowing it. The only way to find out if you have high blood pressure is to have it checked. The bottom number of a blood pressure, called the diastolic pressure, is the measurement during the relaxed phase of the heart's pumping cycle, and if it's consistently 100 or above, you must do something to get it to eighty or below. While a single elevated blood pressure reading doesn't mean you have high blood pressure, it could be a warning sign. Certain diseases, such as kidney disease, can cause high blood pressure. However, in ninety to ninety-five percent of all cases, the cause of high blood pressure is unknown. You can be a calm, relaxed person and still have high blood pressure. Regardless of a person's disposition, it's good to know that reflexology calms and rebalances the sympathetic nervous system. Stimulate the adrenal gland area to regulate the production of adrenaline and promote healthy blood pressure. Work the brain reflex area to open the energy pathways to the brain and help prevent hypertension. Massage the solar plexus to relieve the anxiety caused by hypertension (which, in turn, may contribute to it).

HIGH CHOLESTEROL

Reflex areas: Heart, liver, solar plexus, thyroid

High blood cholesterol is a serious problem because it is a risk factor for heart disease, the number one killer of both men and women in the United States. The higher a person's blood cholesterol, the greater the risk becomes. Note, however, that only one type of cholesterol, LDL cholesterol, acts negatively on the body by building up in artery walls. HDL cholesterol is, by comparison, a positive factor in the blood as it gets rid of LDL.

The reflexology solution is one of regulation. Stimulating the reflex area to the heart improves blood circulation, and stimulating the reflex area to the liver detoxifies the blood, filters toxins, and improves fat digestion. Working on the reflex to the thyroid regulates mineral levels in the body. Lastly, the solar plexus point can help de-stress the body so all systems function better.

HIGH ENERGY/OVERACHIEVERS

Reflex areas: Solar plexus, stomach, brain

Do you feel like you can never do enough? That you must be the best at everything you do and you can't seem to slow down? If you're burning the candle at both ends, you may be a Type-A personality. In your efforts to "be the best that you can be," however, it's easy to overtax your body and mind. While striving to reach your goals is highly regarded in today's society, over-achieving very often leads to stress and anxiety, which can sometimes do more harm than good for the body and soul. A healthy goal for everyone is to take positive action to reduce stress. Working the above reflexology points can calm overachievers' busy minds, help a person slow down, and bring some stress relief from non-stop daily routines.

HYPOGLYCEMIA

Reflex areas: Pituitary, adrenals, thyroid, liver

Have you ever felt shaky when you haven't eaten in a long time? Hypoglycemia, or low blood sugar, is a condition that occurs when levels of glucose in the blood drop too low to fuel the body's activity. Glucose, a form of sugar, is the body's main fuel, and the amount of glucose in the blood is controlled mainly by the hormones insulin and glucagon. Too much or too little of these hormones can cause blood sugar levels to fall too low (hypoglycemia) or rise too high (hyperglycemia). A person with hypoglycemia may feel weak, drowsy, confused, hungry, dizzy, or faint. Other symptoms include headache, paleness, irritability, trembling, sweating, rapid heartbeat, and a cold, clammy feeling. In severe cases, a person can lose consciousness and even lapse into a coma.

Diabetes is often the cause of hypoglycemia. It can also occur in some people under certain conditions such as early pregnancy, prolonged fasting, strenuous exercise, alcoholism, and as a result of certain medications. Diabetes occurs when the body cannot use glucose for fuel because either the pancreas is not able to make enough insulin or the insulin that is available is not effective. As a result, glucose builds up in the blood instead of getting into the body's tissues.

Reflexology can help your body naturally regulate the blood sugar levels and relieve the symptoms of hypoglycemia. Try stimulating the pituitary, adrenals, thyroid, and liver. The pituitary affects energy levels and releases many hormones that affect metabolism, mineral and sugar content in the blood, and fluid retention. The adrenal point helps the body maintain healthy levels of all nutrients and fluids. The liver area encourages a healthy level of glucose absorption (this can prevent hypoglycemia), and working the thyroid area can stabilize blood sugar levels and prevent the "shakes" of a hypoglycemic episode.

IMMUNITY PROBLEMS

Reflex areas: Thymus, spleen, pituitary, brain

A healthy immune system is the cornerstone of good general health. If you're healthy and your immune system is strong, you can interact with germs and not get infections, with allergens and not have allergic reactions, and with carcinogens and not get cancer. If your immune system is weak, you may fall prey to every cold and virus that comes along.

The functions of the immune system are intricate, involving the thymus, spleen, pituitary, hypothalamus, and many other tissues and glands. Problems arise from either under-activity, which can lead to the growth of infections and cancer, and over-activity, which can lead to allergies and autoimmune disorders. The essential responsibility of the immune system is to recognize and protect itself from any materials that do not belong in the body, including abnormal and damaged components. Reflexology can be a partner to this system, strengthening it so that every part of the body can function properly.

To accomplish this partnership, work the thymus area to boost immunity and invigorate your body. Stimulate the spleen area to strengthen the immune system and effectively open up channels of energy to encourage natural healing. Next, move to the pituitary region to maintain a healthy and stable immune system. Finally, massage the reflex area to the brain to improve the immune system's ability to recognize and get rid of foreign entities in the body and to prevent autoimmune disorders, which occur when the immune system mistakenly attacks the body's own tissues.

INFERTILITY

Reflex areas: Hypothalamus, reproductive organs, solar plexus, spine

Almost everyone knows at least one family member, co-worker, or friend who has trouble conceiving. According to the National Center for Health Statistics (NCHS), approximately 4.5 million couples experience infertility each year. Fortunately, in ninety percent of all cases there is a specific cause for the infertility that can be uncovered by physicians who specialize in reproductive medicine. There are several effective treatment methods for most infertility problems, and with appropriate medical diagnosis and treatment, over half of infertile couples will conceive their own children.

Coupling the medical treatment with reflexology can help Mother Nature along! Stimulate the reflex areas to the reproductive organs in both men and women to strengthen the whole reproductive system. This unblocks any areas of congestion so that energy flows freely. Next, work the reflex to the hypothalamus by stimulating the big toe on both feet. This regulates the autonomic nervous system and balances emotions (infertility can be a very emotional issue).

To relax the entire body, stimulate the reflex areas to the solar plexus and the spine, which may be tight from emotional and mental stress. When the body is relaxed, energy flows more smoothly and all systems function more efficiently.

INFLAMMATION (SWELLING)

Reflex areas: Adrenals, thymus, spleen

If you've ever sprained your ankle and watched in horror as it swelled to three times its size, you know about inflammation. Inflammation is the body's normal response to injury and infection, and it is a major element in the healing process. When your body is harmed, its immune, circulatory, and hormonal systems work together to boost the efficiency of the body's defenses and speed the repair of damaged tissue. The redness, warmth, swelling, and pain that occur after an injury are the body's inflammatory reactions, and are evidence that all of these systems are working properly. However, inflammation can become a disease when it persists beyond its normal limits and serves no purpose. In these cases, doctors treat the inflammation with anti-inflammatory drugs, which suppress it, but can be toxic. Reflexology is a natural alternative or add-on to these treatments.

Stimulate the adrenals to release the body's own anti-inflammatory hormone which can help speed recovery from injuries and infections. Work the thymus to boost your immune system and strengthen the body's ability to repair damaged tissue. Finally, massage the spleen to allow the body's electric impulses to bring natural healing to the area of the inflammation.

INSOMNIA

Reflex areas: Brain, thyroid, pineal, pituitary, solar plexus

Every day, millions of people walk around tired and irritable due to lack of sleep. Whether it's difficulty falling asleep, waking frequently during the night with an inability to fall back to sleep, waking too early in the morning, or simply not feeling refreshed by sleep, most people at some time suffer from some form of insomnia. Individuals differ in the amount of sleep they need to feel refreshed. Therefore, insomnia is not defined by the number of hours of sleep a person gets or how long it takes to fall asleep.

Insomnia can be transient (short term), intermittent (on and off), or chronic (constant). It can be caused by many common conditions including being over the age of sixty, stress, outside noise, extreme temperatures, changes in your environment, and problems with your sleep/wake schedule such as jet lag, medication side effects, and depression. Other rare possible causes include arthritis, kidney disease, heart failure, asthma, sleep apnea, narcolepsy, restless-leg syndrome, Parkinson's disease, and hyperthyroidism.

Insomnia affects both males and females of all age groups, though it is more common in females (especially after menopause) and in the elderly. Chronic insomnia is more complex and is normally the consequence of a combination of factors, including underlying physical or mental disorders, depression in particular. Reflexology can relax your body and mind so that you can fall asleep, sleep more soundly, sleep longer, and wake up feeling refreshed.

For best results work five reflex areas. Stimulate the brain region to calm the "chatter" in your head and take your mind off the day's worries so you can sleep. Work the pineal gland to promote deeper, longer, more restful sleep and to regulate your sleep/wake cycle. Move to the pituitary gland area to rebalance your energy, which improves relaxation. Massage the thyroid to stabilize hormone production so you can sleep, and finally, work on the solar plexus area to decrease stress and relax body, mind, and soul.

Jet lag

Reflex areas: Brain, pineal, pituitary, spine

The symptoms of jet lag are numerous. They include disorientation, becoming irrational or unreasonable, being worn out and tired for days after arriving, and a lack of concentration and motivation (especially for any activity that requires effort or skill such as driving, reading, or discussing a business deal). Whether you're a tourist on holiday or traveling for business, jet lag can make everything much more difficult. Not only does it make you feel "off-center," jet lag can also lower your resistance and make you more susceptible to colds, flu, and sore throats. It has also been known to cause dehydration, headaches, dry skin, and nasal irritation.

When you travel into another time zone, your inbuilt circadian rhythms are disturbed, and it can take several days for the body to readjust to the change. NASA estimates that you need one day for every time zone crossed to regain normal rhythm and energy levels. So a five-hour time difference means you will require five days to get back to normal! Do you have that kind of time to recover? Most people don't. Reflexology can help ease your transition into the new time zone and soothe the effects of jet lag away.

There are four reflex points to focus on for alleviating jet lag. Start with the brain area to keep your mind sharp and focused. Next is the pineal gland, which is responsible for producing melatonin, the body's natural hormone for regulating sleep. Working this reflex can help get you back to normal as quickly as possible. Third, work the pituitary to improve overall energy levels. Finally, stimulate the spine area to relax your entire back and neck, which may be tense from sitting on a plane for many hours.

Kidney problems

Reflex areas: Kidneys, bladder, ureters, spine (lower back), thymus

The kidneys are two of the most important organs in your body, and when something goes wrong with them it can be quite dangerous. The kidneys are responsible for regulating body water and the levels of electrolytes, including sodium, calcium, potassium, glucose, phosphorus, chloride, and amino acids in the bloodstream. They also filter toxins and waste products out of the body. Unfortunately, there is no diagnostic test to differentiate between a kidney infection and an infection of the urinary tract (See also urinary tract infections, page 129). The sign of a kidney infection can be determined by the symptoms, which include burning during urination, increase in frequency of urination, urgency, high fever, lower back pain, chills, nausea, vomiting, and diarrhea. If you have any of these symptoms, your doctor will typically take a urine sample for analysis and if there is an infection, will prescribe antibiotics designed to fight the type of bacteria present. Kidney infections result when bacteria travel up the urethra, to the bladder, and then continue up the ureters to the kidneys. Kidney disease, on the other hand, may be hereditary, autoimmune-related, or the result of infection, injury, or hypertension. If kidney problems are not treated, the kidneys can stop functioning properly and go into failure, which can be fatal. To prevent kidney problems, it is beneficial to avoid kidney stressors, which include smoking, high blood pressure, dehydration, alcohol, caffeine and other stimulants, and a high-protein diet. And, of course, add a little reflexology to this common sense approach!

Work the kidneys to promote balanced elimination of the body's water and waste, and strengthen the kidneys. Follow with the bladder to help the body process toxins, encourage elimination, and prevent bacteria from reaching the kidneys. Massage the ureters so that they can better fight bacteria and prevent the development of a UTI or kidney infection. From here, move to the spine for some relief from the pain and burning, and the thymus area to boost your immune system so that your body can fight the bacteria that causes kidney problems.

KNEE PROBLEMS

Reflex areas: Knee, spine, adrenals

Your knee joint is the largest joint in your body and, perhaps one of the most versatile and complex. This amazing structure of muscles, bones, ligaments, and cartilage supports and stabilizes your body as you bend, straighten, and twist during daily activities. The knee joint, however, is one of the most vulnerable joints in the body and after years of repetitive weight-bearing, may begin to show signs of aging or wear and tear. Whether it's a result of genetics, injury or simply the constant weight of your body on your knee, pain and swelling in the knee is a well-known problem, especially in athletes and weekend warriors. The most common conditions that affect the knee are osteoarthritis, chondromalacia, bursitis, popliteal cyst, tendonitis, and torn cartilage. If you have any of these painful problems, reflexology can help ease some of the pain and strengthen the knee area to prevent even more damage.

There are three reflex points to pay attention to for knee trouble. First is the knee region itself in order to strengthen the knee joint and to send healing energy to any injured areas. Second is the spine because it bears the main support for your entire body, taking some weight off the knees. Last is the adrenal gland area that increases the body's natural anti-inflammatory hormones, which soothe problematic knees.

LIVER PROBLEMS

Reflex areas: Liver, lungs, small intestine

The liver is the "great filter of the body," as it is responsible for detoxifying the blood and processing nutrients. This major organ breaks down fatty acids, converts glucose to a storage form of energy called glycogen, and decides whether incoming substances are useful to the body or waste. Liver disorders are caused when liver cells are damaged by alcoholism, too much iron, infection, or disease. If your liver is stressed, you may experience symptoms such as diarrhea, nausea, low fever, mood swings, and skin breakouts. An underactive liver may produce symptoms that include anemia, fatigue, mood swings, constipation, poor digestion, body aches, and insomnia.

Cirrhosis of the liver is a serious condition, characterized by severe scarring, that may develop after years of chronic liver disease. A healthy liver is normally able to replace most liver cells that are damaged by alcohol. However, in individuals with cirrhosis, the liver is unable to replace them.

Reflexology can strengthen the liver so that it can function properly. It rebalances energy, and helps your body process and eliminate the toxins that are making your liver sluggish. To accomplish this, focus on three reflex areas: the liver, lungs, and small intestine. Working these three areas together detoxify the system, improve the liver's condition, and motivate a positive absorption of nutrients, while also encouraging proper elimination of waste matter.

LOW ENERGY/LACK OF MOTIVATION

Reflex areas: Brain, thymus, pituitary, thyroid

Everybody goes through periods in their life when they reevaluate what they want and in which direction they want to proceed. Sometimes, this reflection and introspection can be very difficult and can lead to confusion about what direction to take due to stress and low self-esteem, lack of motivation, addictions (chemical, behavioral, and others), relationship breakdown, grief, and loss. Conversely, these problems can also be the impetus that causes you to reevaluate your life and turn inward. If you are experiencing low energy and a lack of motivation, reflexology applied to the above points can help renew your hopes and dreams, and motivate you to get up every day and face the world with a smile.

MENOPAUSE

Reflex areas: Sex organs (ovaries, uterus, fallopian tubes), solar plexus, thyroid, brain

Menopause is a condition that millions of women go through as they get older and their bodies adjust to hormonal changes, particularly declining estrogen levels. Menopausal women may experience hot flashes, mood swings, insomnia, and vaginal dryness. While these symptoms are annoying, they are not life-threatening. Many women go through this change of life with minimal discomfort. But there are other women who are more disturbed by menopause, and turn to hormone replacement therapy as a scientific treatment for uncomfortable symptoms.

If you or someone you know is going through menopause or is experiencing post-menopausal symptoms, reflexology can bring a welcome relief to some of the discomforts. It is also a hands-on way to ease yourself through the changes in your body. The three reflex points for these symptoms are those associated with female sex organs, specifically the uterus, ovaries, and fallopian tubes. Stimulating these areas sends healing energy throughout the body that can ease a lot of the stress that goes with erratic hormonal shifts.

Additionally, you'll want to work the solar plexus to return a sense of harmony, and the thyroid to regulate blood sugar levels, improve your sex drive, and rebalance overall energy. Also, work the brain area to help soothe the normal anxiety and stress that accompanies the transition into this new phase of life. Menopause should not signify the end of your youth and sexuality, but rather the beginning of a new and exciting chapter of your life.

MIGRAINES

(See also headaches)

Reflex areas: Brain, pituitary, eyes, stomach, solar plexus

As someone who gets them every so often, I can tell you that a migraine is one of the most painful and debilitating disorders I have ever experienced. More than just a painful headache, a migraine usually brings with it many other dreadful symptoms, including nausea, vomiting, and sensitivity to light and sound. You can distinguish a migraine from a regular headache if the pain is on one side of the head, pulses or throbs, or is aggravated by routine physical activity. Migraine attacks seem to increase during periods of hormonal fluctuation, such as during PMS, menstruation, pregnancy, and menopause. The scary thing about migraines is that they can attack at any time, though they often occur in the morning.

Most people who suffer from frequent migraines can tell the warning signs, which include seeing flashing lights, zigzag lines (which is what I get), a blind spot, or having tunnel vision. These visual signs characterize a "migraine with an aura." For many people, the only way to get rid of a migraine, besides taking medication, is to stop everything, lie down in a darkened room, and try to sleep.

While experts believe that serotonin, a chemical in your brain that can constrict blood vessels and stimulate pain receptors, is the main cause of migraines, studies also show that heredity may play a role in this painful disorder. There are several common situations that trigger migraines, including missed meals, psychological stress, fatigue or irregular sleep, changes in weather, and traveling to different altitudes. In addition, particular foods, beverages, and chemicals can trigger migraines, including alcohol, coffee, tea, cola, cheese, chocolate, monosodium glutamate (MSG), nitrates (food preservatives), smoked fish, nuts, and pickled foods.

If you suffer from migraines, the best thing you can do for yourself is to recognize the warning signs and try to relax before the migraine hits. Reflexology can help to relieve stress and calm your body before and during a migraine. More importantly, regular reflexology can even help prevent future migraine attacks.

As with so many other problems, working a combination of reflex points seems to be the key to success. Work the brain to decrease anxiety and regulate the production of serotonin. Stimulate the pituitary point to balance out the body's chemicals, some of which can cause migraines when they are low or high. Massage the eye area to get rid of some of that throbbing pain and straighten out any vision-associated side effects. If you're feeling sick to your stomach, work that point too, along with the solar plexus to maintain a more balanced mental state, which keeps you calmer and eases the migraine more quickly.

MOTION SICKNESS

Reflex areas: Stomach, ears, eyes

If you've ever been on a boat that is being tossed back and forth by the waves, on an airplane experiencing heavy turbulence, or stuck in the backseat of a poorly ventilated car, you probably have experienced a form of motion sickness. This common disorder occurs when the body is subjected to movement in different directions, while visual contact with the actual outside horizon is lost. The balance center of the inner ear then sends information to the brain which conflicts with the visual information of apparently standing still in the interior cabin of a boat, airplane, or automobile. This is why people always tell you to stay on the deck of a boat, where you can see the horizon.

If you suffer from motion sickness, you may experience symptoms that include dizziness, fatigue, and nausea, which may progress to vomiting. Fear and anxiety can increase these symptoms. There are several over-the-counter and prescription drugs that are available to prevent or limit the symptoms. However, you can also prevent motion sickness by facing forward and looking outside at the horizon, finding areas where there is lesser movement on a boat or plane, and of course by using reflexology. Reflexology balances your energy, soothes nausea and dizziness, and may even prevent motion sickness from beginning.

To accomplish this, work the stomach point, especially to curb nausea. Move to the ear area to regain a sense of balance, and stimulate the reflex area to the eyes on both feet to strengthen your eyesight and to ensure that the visual information does not conflict with the information from the ear. Additionally, you can work the reflexology area to the brain to improve your sense of mental focus.

MULTIPLE SCLEROSIS

(see also autoimmune disorders)

Reflex areas: Adrenals, thymus, thyroid, brain, spine

Multiple sclerosis (MS) is one of the most mysterious of all diseases. Little is known about the causes and factors that influence its development. Considered to be an autoimmune disease, MS occurs when the body's immune system attacks and scars the myelin, which is the fatty layer of protective insulation that surrounds nerve fibers. This results in interference with the nerve impulses and a disturbance of body functions, which leads to muscle weakness, vision disorders, loss of motor strength and coordination, and loss of bowel and bladder control. The course of MS varies. Some people experience severe symptoms that eventually lead to paralysis, while others may experience alternating cycles of intense disturbance and remission, and still other people experience only a few symptoms at the beginning and never have them again. Actually, more than seventy-five percent of people with MS will never have to use a wheelchair.

In addition to problems with autoimmunity, the onset of MS is also linked to viruses, which may somehow trigger the body's immune reaction. Currently, there are some conventional and alternative therapies that help to increase nerve-cell activity and slow the course of this disease. Lifestyle changes including an improved diet, regular exercise, and stress management can also help to enhance health and lessen the symptoms of MS. Reflexology's role here is to help boost the immune system and optimize the body's ability to heal.

In focusing on the immune system, first we work the adrenal glands to strengthen the entire endocrine system. From here, work the pineal gland as an overall tonic. Next work the pituitary point to regulate metabolism, sugars, and the body's energy levels, all of which are often affected directly or indirectly by MS. You will also want to stimulate the spine region, which can be irritated by this disease, the thymus to improve the body's ability to defend itself against viruses that may trigger MS, and the thyroid to promote a healthy chemical and emotional balance.

NAUSEA

Reflex areas: Stomach, small intestine, inner ear, brain

"Barf, spew, spit up, throw up, gag, retch, heave, puke, upchuck, toss one's cookies, spiff one's biscuits." These are all ways to colorfully describe the awful act of vomiting, brought on by nausea. Nausea and vomiting occur when the vomiting center in the brain senses a variety of problems. This causes the windpipe to close up and the abdominal wall and diaphragm muscles to tighten suddenly and forcefully. Consequently, the stomach ejects any food or fluid up and out of the esophagus.

Children, especially infants, have more problems with vomiting since they have a lower threshold in the vomiting center. If it continues for a long time, nausea and vomiting can cause severe dehydration, and can be a sign of a more serious illness. Reflexology relieves the unpleasant feeling of nausea, calms the vomiting center in the brain, and helps prevent you from "losing your lunch."

The best four areas to work for nausea include the stomach (obviously), the small intestine for proper elimination of wastes, the brain to calm the vomiting center, and the ears, which can contribute to feeling green.

NECK PAIN

Reflex areas: Neck, spine, adrenals, solar plexus

What a pain in the neck! Whether it's mildly annoying or so severe that it's unbearable and incapacitating, almost everyone experiences some sort of neck pain or stiffness at one time or another. Most complaints of neck pain are minor, commonly caused by holding your head in an awkward position for too long while working, watching TV, using a computer, reading a book, or talking on the phone. In these cases, the joints in your neck can "lock" and the neck muscles become painfully fatigued. Fortunately, most minor, posture-induced neck pain disappears after rest and some gentle stretching. However, neck pain that lasts for several days or frequently returns is a signal that something isn't right and requires medical attention.

The neck (cervical spine) is composed of seven vertebrae that begin in the upper torso and end at the base of the skull. These vertebrae, along with the ligaments (like thick rubber bands), provide stability to the spine and muscles and allow for support and motion. The neck has a significant amount of motion and supports the weight of the head. If the muscles that support your head are not kept strong and in good condition, the upper part of your spinal column is vulnerable to strains and injuries. Because the neck is less protected than the rest of the spine, it is more susceptible to injury and disorders that produce pain and restrict motion.

Reflexology can help to strengthen the energy in the neck and soothe neck aches, pains and stiffness. Beginning with the neck point (which strengthens the neck), move to working the spine to support the neck and bring overall healing energy to that area. Next move to the adrenal glands to achieve a natural anti-inflammatory response. Finally, stimulate the solar plexus to improve your overall sense of calm, since many people carry tension in their necks.

OSTEOPOROSIS

Reflex areas: Adrenals, heart, pituitary, small intestine

Osteoporosis is a major public health threat for more than twenty-eight million Americans, eighty percent of which are women. In the U.S. today, ten million individuals already have the disease and eighteen million more have low bone mass, placing them at increased risk for osteoporosis. The scary news is that one in two women and one in eight men over age fifty will have an osteoporosis-related fracture in their lifetime. While osteoporosis is often thought of as an older person's disease, it can strike at any age.

Osteoporosis, or "porous bone," is a disease in which bones deteriorate and become fragile and more likely to break. It is often called the silent disease, because bone loss occurs without symptoms. People may not know that they have osteoporosis until their bones become so weak that a sudden strain, bump, or fall causes a fracture or a vertebra to collapse. Broken bones, also known as fractures, occur typically in the hip, spine, and wrist.

Reflexology can strengthen your body and protect it from this degenerative, "silent" disease. Stimulate the reflex area to the adrenals to regulate metabolism. Also work the reflex area to the heart to improve circulation of blood and oxygen to every cell of the body, the reflex area to the pituitary gland to regulate the mineral and sugar contents of the blood, and the reflex area to the small intestine to improve the body's absorption of nutrients.

PREMENSTRUAL SYNDROME (PMS)

Reflex areas: Sex organs (uterus, ovaries, fallopian tubes), brain, thyroid, stomach, solar plexus

Approximately ninety percent of all menstruating women between the ages of twenty and fifty experience the symptoms of Premenstrual Syndrome (PMS) regularly. Although there are over one hundred and fifty different symptoms, the most common are irritability, frustration, headaches, bloating, mood swings, weight gain, vertigo, marital strife, depression, exhaustion, loss of sex drive, anger, panic, backaches, fatigue, and breast swelling and tenderness. These symptoms occur before menstruation and usually cease with the onset of a period. PMS is common in women who live in technologically advanced countries. Since there are numerous cultures among which this condition is essentially non-existent and unknown, researchers believe that diet, stress, and foreign estrogens, often introduced in the form of contraceptives, are all major contributors to this disorder.

Reflexology can relieve the symptoms of PMS and restore balance to your body and mind. It can help calm those mood swings that make you do and say "crazy" things. Particularly, focus on your sex organs region to even out hormone levels, the stomach to alleviate cramps, the thyroid to tone down mood swings, and the solar plexus to restore harmony. Finally, stimulate the brain reflex point to prevent PMS from disturbing your happiness.

PSORIASIS

Reflex areas: Small intestine, kidneys, liver, thyroid

Itchy, flaky, dry, red, inflamed skin. Ever seen or had it? That is usually psoriasis, which is a common skin disorder. Psoriasis is the growth of too many skin cells. While a normal skin cell matures in twenty-eight to thirty days, a psoriatic skin cell takes only three to six days. Though not contagious, psoriasis can look quite menacing. Appearing most commonly on the scalp, knees, elbows, hands, and feet, it rarely affects the face. There are several forms of psoriasis, but "plaque psoriasis," which is characterized by inflamed lesions topped with silvery white scales, is the most common.

The symptoms of psoriasis can range from mild to moderate to very severe and disabling. Some people who have psoriasis experience spontaneous remissions, but no one knows why this happens and they are unfortunately unpredictable. Both men and women get psoriasis, and it can strike at any age, but most often between fifteen and thirty-five. No one knows exactly what causes psoriasis, although a recent study has established that it is an immune-mediated disorder. Other factors that may trigger the onset of psoriasis are heredity, physical trauma to the skin, infections, and stress. Unfortunately, there is no cure for psoriasis, but there are many different topical and systemic treatments that can suppress it for periods of time. Reflexology helps prevent future breakouts and relieve the discomfort of psoriasis.

The reflex points for psoriasis include the kidneys, liver, and small intestine, to eliminate toxins that could cause this condition. Additionally, work the thyroid for chemical balance, adrenals to decrease stress-related psoriasis, and the solar plexus to restore calm.

SCIATICA

(See also page 74, Sciatic nerve)

SEXUAL PROBLEMS

Sex is everywhere—in advertisements for cigarettes, automobiles, and fast-food restaurants. In short, sex sells. Within everyone there exists a dynamic drive for reproducing the human species that motivates much of our everyday behavior. For some people, the sex drive is so intense that it rates second only to oxygen for survival requirements! It is one of the strongest animal drives, and it cannot be ignored.

For those experiencing problems in the sexual arena, help is here! Reflexology offers drug-free relief for sluggish or diminishing sex drives by stimulating the reflex areas that are directly responsible for the overall health and the well-being of the body, increasing your sex drive and hormone production, and slowing the aging process.

Reflexology can also bring enhanced "touch" into a relationship, which is important to intimacy and the development of a deep emotional connection. All couples must learn to communicate their desires and feelings to each other in every aspect of their lives. In the sexual arena, communication is the key to happiness. Reflexology can help couples learn to communicate honestly with each other and be sensitive to a partner's feelings. Reflexology is also a great way to spice up your sex life by learning how to tune into each other's body and provide intimate physical pleasure.

The reflexology points for sexual problems vary by problem. Those experiencing a low sex drive will want to focus on endocrine glands (including the thyroid, pituitary, pineal, thymus, adrenals, ovaries, and testes) which are responsible for secreting hormones and releasing them into the body. Of these, the thyroid and adrenals are the most important to boost your sex drive and improve sexual functioning for both men and women. Additionally, stimulating the reflex areas for sexual organs strengthens both the organ itself, as well as your sex drive.

Those struggling with the problem of impotency can use reflexology to help restore these important abilities and improve the levels of testosterone in the body. In this case, working the adrenal glands, pituitary, thyroid, and sex organs is recommended as well as the prostate, testes, and vas deferens.

For prostate problems, stimulate adrenal glands to produce an adequate amount of hormones, the sex organs, the bladder (to eliminate toxins), and the ureters to prevent infections. On the other hand, if you find your sex life is affected by stress, then you'll want to work the solar plexus and brain—not just for yourself but for your partner! Stimulating the solar plexus area is a great way to calm down, and working the brain center restores mental and physical harmony for all parties.

SINUS PROBLEMS

Reflex areas: sinuses, lungs, pituitary

Having trouble breathing? Sinusitis is a disorder that causes great misery. Your sinuses, which are located behind your cheekbones and forehead and around your eyes, normally drain almost a quart of mucus every day in order to keep the air you breath moistened. However, if they are infected and swollen, your sinuses can't drain properly. Sinus infections can be quite uncomfortable with symptoms that include head congestion, nasal congestion and discharge (usually yellowish-green), pain and tenderness over the facial sinuses, pain in the upper jaw, recurrent headaches, and fever. They're caused by a variety of things including hay fever, smoke, a nasal deformity (such as a deviated septum) or sinuses that don't drain well, an abscess in an upper tooth, sneezing hard with your mouth closed, or blowing your nose too much when you have a cold. Reflexology can help to strengthen the body so it can naturally clear the infection and reduce congestion. Begin by working the sinus reflex point on both feet. Next, work the lungs and pituitary. This combination often brings fast relief and deters associated headaches.

SMOKING

Reflex areas: Brain, lungs, solar plexus

Anyone who has ever tried to quit smoking knows just how hard it can be. A motivating factor for quitting is not only the health risk that smoking poses, but also the fact that second-hand smoke is a definite health hazard to both adults and children. Every year, smoking causes several thousand cases of asthma attacks, inner ear infections, bronchitis, pneumonia, and lower chest infections. In 1992, the Environmental Protection Agency identified it as a direct cause of cancer. Sometimes it can take years for the results of smoke exposure to surface. For example, there is strong evidence that second-hand smoke causes some obstruction and hardening of the arteries. This often does not show up for several years, however, and then suddenly someone discovers they have high blood pressure due to regularly inhaling passive smoke.

Reflexology can support an individual's decision to try to quit smoking. Stimulate the reflex area to the solar plexus when you begin to crave nicotine. Stimulating the reflex area to the lungs improves breathing, as well as helping the lungs draw in the proper amount of oxygen to feed the brain. Working the reflex to the brain sends healing signals to the area that is craving "a smoke" and strengthens your pledge to stop smoking. Better still, reflexology gives you something to do with your hands rather than hold a cigarette!

SNORING PROBLEMS (SLEEP APNEA)

Reflex areas: Adrenals, lungs, spleen

Have you ever been awakened by your own snoring? If so, then you may have a problem with sleep apnea, which is related to physical obstructive breathing during sleep. Snoring occurs when the muscles of the palate, the uvula, and sometimes the tonsils relax during deep sleep and act as vibrating noise-makers when the air of breathing moves across them. Excessively bulky tissue in the back of the throat as it narrows into the airways, as well as a long palate and/or uvula, can also contribute to snoring.

Obstructive sleep apnea, a serious and sometimes fatal condition, is diagnosed when loud snoring is interrupted by episodes of completely obstructed breathing. This occurs when the airway in the back of the throat collapses and prevents oxygen from entering the lungs and reaching your bloodstream. The effect of these obstructed breathing episodes is reduced blood oxygen levels to the brain, which forces the snorer to stay in a lighter state of sleep so that the breathing passage muscles are kept tighter. This prevents the snorer from getting restful sleep and can lead to a tendency to drift off during daytime hours—on the job, or worse, at the wheel of a car. Central sleep apnea is a more rare form of the disease that occurs when the brain fails to signal the lungs to breathe.

It's no joke, snoring can be dangerous (and not just because it frustrates your mate). The National Council on Sleep Disorders attributes 38,000 cardiovascular deaths a year to sleep apnea. In addition, the decreased levels of oxygen in the blood during sleep can cause or contribute to high blood pressure, strokes, fluid retention, and abnormal heartbeats.

Reflexology can help prevent snoring from becoming a more dangerous condition. And that's good news for everyone, especially partners of snorers! To deter snoring, work the adrenal glands to release anti-inflammatory hormones, the lungs to improve breathing, the brain, and the spleen, which is responsible for excess blood during emergencies, when oxygen in the circulatory system is short (as it is for sleep apnea sufferers).

SWOLLEN ANKLES AND FEET

Reflex areas: Adrenals, bladder, kidneys, ureters

Have you ever waked with your feet and ankles perfectly fine, but by the end of the day they were swollen and your shoes were painful? This swelling is the result of a buildup of fluids in your skin tissue. During the day, gravity pulls the fluids to your feet and ankles, causing them to swell. Edema is another kind of swelling, which is caused by a pooling of lymphatic fluid in the ankles and wrists. If you suffer from edema, the swollen areas may be tender and sometimes painful. Massage is not recommended for edema.

For many pregnant women, swollen ankles and feet affect them throughout pregnancy. During pregnancy, feet change in volume by as much as twenty five percent, largely due to fluid retention and increased blood volume. To reduce swelling, doctors often advise cutting back on sodium, which can cause fluid retention, and maintaining proper body weight, since excess weight can slow the circulation of body fluids and put extra pressure on your veins, causing fluid buildup.

Reflexology can help swelling by improving circulation and decreasing or preventing fluid retention. Stimulating the reflex area to the adrenals normalizes the energy flow in the body. Working on reflex areas to the bladder, kidneys, and ureters strengthens the body's urinary system and promotes proper elimination. This, in turn, can prevent edema.

TENDONITIS

Reflex areas: Adrenals, Achilles tendon

If you do too much stair climbing or bicycle riding, you run the risk of developing tendonitis, which is a painful condition that involves the back of your heel, otherwise known as the Achilles tendon. Tendonitis, which is caused by overuse of this tendon, is the inflammation or small tears in the hard, inelastic cords that attach your thigh muscle to your lower leg. The Achilles tendon can become inflamed and damaged from many movements including pronation (inward tilting of the heel) or supination (outward tilting of the heel); excessive weight; over-use, such as running or tennis or other sport activities; and sometimes metabolic problems, such as diabetes or arthritis.

Women who frequently wear high heels (generally over one inch high) may develop "shortened Achilles tendons" and experience pain when they try to go down to a lower-heeled shoe. For this, pain can be relieved through stretching. Reflexology's role in aiding this condition is to strengthen the Achilles tendon and ease pain and inflammation. Start by stimulating the adrenal glands to reduce swelling, then move to the Achilles tendon region to speed healing.

THYROID PROBLEMS

Reflex areas: Thyroid, neck, solar plexus

Since the thyroid gland controls so many aspects of our metabolism, any disturbance in its function can produce symptoms in almost every system of the body. The thyroid has the unique ability to concentrate iodine and use it to manufacture "thyroid hormone," which affects metabolism. When the thyroid is overactive, it causes weight loss, insomnia, hand tremors (shakes), palpitations, bulging of the eyes (exophthalmus), heat intolerance, and digestive disturbances. Note that hyperthyroidism usually requires conventional treatment with drugs or surgery.

If the thyroid is under active, which is more common, the result is hypothyroidism. Elevated cholesterol, weight gain, and what seems to be generally slower behavior characterizes this disease. The treatment of hypothyroidism is generally accomplished by replacing the normal thyroid hormone with a synthetic hormone. Unfortunately, thyroid function tests are not reliable and they sometimes indicate that people have a normal thyroid balance when they do not.

Reflexology helps regulate the thyroid's production of thyroid hormone and can balance your metabolism. The three key areas for this include the thyroid point itself, followed by the neck area (which is where the thyroid gland is located), and the solar plexus reflex area, which serves to sooth a disrupted nervous system.

TOOTHACHE

Reflex areas: Sinuses, neck, brain, adrenals

Toothaches can be excruciating. If you've ever had one, you probably take better care of your teeth now than ever before. Toothaches can have a number of different causes, including decay, gum problems, abscesses, loose fillings, exposed tooth roots, cracked, broken and missing fillings, or cracked teeth. In addition, a toothache may be caused by habits like tooth-"grinding", which people commonly to do at night, or sinus infections. Frequently, toothaches are caused by germs that enter the live part of the tooth through a decayed area, a loose filling, a crack in the tooth, or by a nerve exposure following an accident. It is usually very difficult for people to tell which tooth is actually causing pain because of the type of nerve supply in teeth.

Whichever tooth it is and whatever the cause may be, you should see your dentist. In the interim, reflexology can help effectively relieve the pain of a toothache. Work the brain area to take your mind off the pain, the neck reflex point if you find your neck is sore from holding your head oddly during a toothache bout, and sinuses to improve circulation to the gum and mouth area. Also work the adrenal reflex point to reduce inflammation in the gums.

ULCERS

Reflex areas: Stomach, thymus, thyroid

Each year, ulcers affect about four million people and more than 40,000 people have surgery because of persistent symptoms or problems from ulcers. About twenty million Americans develop at least one ulcer during their lifetime and about 6,000 people die of ulcer-related complications. An ulcer is a sore or lesion that forms in the lining of the stomach or duodenum where acid and pepsin are present. In general, ulcers in the stomach and duodenum are referred to as peptic ulcers. While people used to believe that stress and diet caused ulcers, research has shown that most ulcers develop as a result of a bacterial infection. Other factors that may contribute to ulcers include cigarettes, foods and beverages containing caffeine, alcohol, and physical stress.

The most common symptom of an ulcer is a gnawing or burning pain in the abdomen. The pain often occurs between meals and in the early hours of the morning, and it may last from a few minutes to a few hours. Less common ulcer symptoms include nausea, vomiting, and a loss of appetite and weight. Sometimes people have a bleeding ulcer, which occurs in the stomach and duodenum, and they don't even know it because the blood loss is slow and blood may not be obvious. They may just feel tired and weak. Doctors now have many ways to diagnose and treat ulcers. Reflexology works hand in hand with physicians by strengthening the stomach to prevent an ulcer from developing, and relieving the painful symptoms of an existing ulcer.

The three areas to focus on for an ulcer are the stomach, to relieve the associated symptoms there, the thymus to boost your immune system, which in turn will fight the bacteria that causes ulcers, and the thyroid to stabilize the levels of acid and pepsin in the stomach.

URINARY TRACT INFECTIONS

(See also Bladder infections)

Reflex areas: Bladder, kidneys, ureters

Urinary tract infections are extremely common—only respiratory infections occur more often. Each year, UTIs account for about eight million doctor-visits. Women are especially prone to UTIs, and one woman in five develops a UTI during her lifetime. Some men do get UTIs and this may be a warning sign of possible prostate trouble. Not everyone with a UTI has symptoms, but most people get at least some. These may include a frequent urge to urinate and a painful, burning feeling in the area of the bladder or urethra during urination. Other symptoms that may indicate a more serious kidney infection include pain in the back or side below the ribs, nausea, or vomiting.

UTIs are normally treated with courses of antibiotics and urinary anesthetics, but these cannot prevent recurrent infections. Reflexology, on the other hand, can help relieve the painful symptoms of UTIs and strengthen the urinary system to prevent future infections. Specifically, stimulate the ureters reflex point to strengthen your entire urinary tract system and build your resistance to infections in that part of the body. Move on to working the bladder to provide support to the entire urinary system. Finally, give some time and attention to the kidney point so that unwanted chemicals that can harm the bladder walls are properly eliminated.

WARTS AND CORNS

Reflex areas: Thymus, pituitary, spleen

Most people, even doctors, often confuse warts and corns because they look alike and occur in the same areas of the feet. Despite their similar appearance, however, they're completely different. Corns only occur on the feet. They are created by constant pressure, and are not contagious. Warts, on the other hand, can appear in all other areas of the body and can be contagious. The most common types are plantar warts (which are flat-surfaced warts that appear on the sole of your foot), common warts (which are hard, round or oval, raised warts that usually appear on your hands), and flat warts (which are slightly darker than the surrounding flesh and are usually seen in children).

Reflexology protects the body from the viruses that can cause warts, and can help strengthen the body to speed up the healing process for both warts and corns. The points essential to this goal are the thymus and pituitary (to boost immunity), and the spleen to open up channels and strengthen the body's natural healing abilities.

WEIGHT PROBLEMS

Reflex areas:

To lose weight: Thyroid, pineal, pituitary, liver, colon, kidneys

To gain weight: Thyroid, solar plexus, stomach, brain

Whether you want to lose weight or gain weight, a key element in both processes is your metabolism. You've probably heard it many times, but do you really know what it is? Metabolism is the body's process of converting food into energy (movement and heat). It takes place in your muscles and organs, as the result of what we commonly refer to as "burning calories". Metabolism is essentially the speed at which your body's motor is running. To lose weight, you must try to increase your metabolism through exercise and diet. To gain weight, which is usually not what most people want to do, you must slow your metabolism through changes in diet and sometimes medications. Reflexology can help you whether you're trying to lose or gain a few pounds. It does so by regulating your metabolism and helping control your appetite.

For those hoping to lose weight, work the thyroid area to boost your metabolism. Also stimulate the pineal gland to suppress an overactive appetite, the pituitary gland to regulate fluid retention, the kidneys for proper elimination, the liver for detoxifying, the colon, and the small intestine. For those wishing to gain weight, focus on the brain reflex point, the solar plexus (to better regulate all organ functions), the stomach to encourage a healthy appetite, and the thyroid to regulate metabolism so your body slows the rate at which it burns calories.

Chapter 6:
Sole Food

OPEN THE GATEWAYS TO HIGHER CONSCIOUSNESS THROUGH YOUR FEET!

PART I:
THE SEVEN CHAKRAS

· ·

Every reflex area that you'll find on your feet corresponds to a specific chakra. And just what is a chakra you ask? In the next few pages you'll find out. To get the most out of a reflexology session, it's useful to understand the significance of each chakra center and how it can enhance your healing potential. By familiarizing yourself with the power inherent in each of the seven chakras, you can begin to understand the connections between the body, mind, spirit, disease, and healing. Through your feet, you can also realize the connection between your thoughts and your health, your mind and your body.

I was intuitively guided to integrate the use of reflexology with all the other modalities the universe sends through me, and found that the spiritual aspects of this form of work were as exact and powerful as the physical. For example, if a person were having great difficulty communicating something, the Throat chakra reflex point of the foot would be sore and tender. Or, if a person were having problems with relationships, the Heart chakra reflex points on the foot would reflect that. There have been cases where a spontaneous release of suppressed expression has occurred simply by working these reflexes. When I've worked the throat reflex, people have simply "exploded" in verbal release of something they needed to say. When I've worked the heart reflex, several people have actually felt a wave of emotion sweep over them, and one person even started to cry. With this in mind, I'm presenting these concepts to you for consideration in your own exploration of reflexology. I believe you will find this approach a wonderful adjunct that provides even more options for how you use reflexology to make your life happier and healthier.

WHAT IS A CHAKRA?

A chakra is an area of interconnection between the body and the spirit. To understand the reflex-chakra connection, it helps to first understand the basics of energy centers in the body. *Chakra* is a Sanskrit word that means "wheels of light." These "wheels" are energy centers in the body, each of which has a purpose and associations with various aspects of body, mind, and spirit. Carl Jung referred to the chakras as the "gateways of consciousness." According to metaphysicians, every chakra also has a spiritual lesson that we must learn in order adopt a higher consciousness. In Eastern religious traditions, it is believed that every body has seven primary chakras that make up the human energy system.

Researchers have actually been able to confirm the existence of seven chakras and map out their locations in the body with precision through the use of a sophisticated, non-invasive scanner that simply listens to the body's radiant frequencies. From these scans, it appears that each chakra is a flattened funnel shape that is no larger than one-eighth of an inch in diameter. Often symbolized as lotus flowers, chakras appear as wheels of pure, radiant energy that spin at great speeds. How open or closed these wheels are, and the rate and direction of spin, is often indicative of wellness (or disease) in body, mind, and spirit.

WHERE ARE THEY LOCATED?

The seven chakras are located in a linear pathway within the body, between the base of the spine and the top of the head. Similar to the way that the soles of your feet show a mini map of the entire body, all body parts are represented along the chakra pathway. The chakra system begins with the Root chakra at the base of the spine. As energy becomes higher in frequency, it moves up to a higher chakra. The highest vibrations of energy correspond to the Crown chakra, at the top of the head and the top of the chakra system. Here are the locations of each chakra in the body:

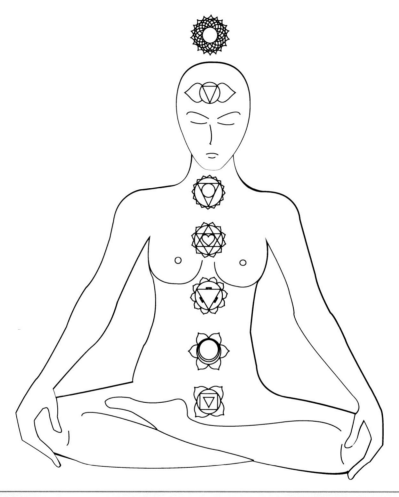

CHAKRAS	LOCATION
Root	at the base of spine
Lower Abdomen	just above genital area
Solar Plexus	in the center of the body
Heart	in the center of the chest, two to three inches above Solar Plexus
Throat	in the throat, between the collar bones
Third Eye	between the eyes
Crown	at the top and center of the head

What do they do?

The seven chakras function as your body's antenna, reaching out and receiving a wide variety of energetic information. This information may or may not be used by the body. Think of your body as the focal point through which waves or electric vibrations are able to pass. Every part vibrates with a different frequency of energy, and each chakra rotates at a speed that corresponds to the different frequencies in specific parts of the body; the higher chakras spin faster than the lower ones. Each chakra is attached to one of the seven endocrine glands of the body and is represented by a specific color. By focusing on the color that is associated with each chakra, you can actually affect that energy center through color therapy.

Color Therapy

Color therapy is a form of energy healing. It can be administered in several different ways, including staring at a specific color, soaking in a tinted bath, wearing a certain color, or having color applied to acupressure points with colored rods or colored beams of light. Color therapy is based on the fact that color is light energy, and each color expresses a range of frequencies for specific wavelengths of light. Since the chakras themselves are vibrations of energy, it makes sense that each of them has a specific color. There are four theories on how color therapy works:

Theory #1: Some researchers claim that light promotes the binding of neurotransmitters to receptors, which can combat depression.

Theory #2: Wavelengths of colors can alter brain waves, thus allowing patients to access subconscious emotions that may cause illnesses.

Theory #3: Chinese medicine believes that disease is caused by an imbalance of energy, and therefore different colors (wavelengths) can restore a balance of energy.

Theory #4: Color wavelengths travel along the optic nerve and enter the brain's pituitary gland, which signals other endocrine glands to secrete hormones that can either stimulate or calm the body.

Color therapy has worked for me because I know that when I am surrounded by certain colors I feel very different emotions. When I am tense and irritable from the stress of daily life, spending time in a room that is painted in soothing shades of lavender or pale blue always relaxes me and makes me feel calmer. On the other hand, when I want to feel a burst of energy, I will wear a vibrant orange or red shirt that makes me feel happy and alive. A yellow kitchen always seems sunny and joyful and I light my green candle when I want to open my heart and express my feelings in relationships. I've even heard that an orange-colored bathroom can encourage better elimination!

On the Reflexology Sox™, the reflex areas are colored to correspond with the appropriate chakra color. As you stimulate each area, you can focus your eyes on the color and reveal all the spiritual and emotional aspects of that chakra's color. In the Chakra system, the colors appear in the same order as the colors of the rainbow. Red is the lowest frequency at the base chakra and white/gold is the highest frequency (crown). So, as energy moves upward in the chakra system, it changes color and eventually becomes white light. See chart below:

CHAKRA	COLOR	ASSOCIATED REFLEX AREAS
Root Chakra	Red	Colon, Hemorrhoids, Lymph system, Spine
Lower Abdomen Chakra	Orange	Appendix, Bladder, Duodenum, Hips, Ileocecal valve, Sciatica, Sex organs, Ureters
Solar Plexus Chakra	Yellow	Adrenals, Gallbladder, Kidneys, Liver, Pancreas, Solar plexus, Spleen, Stomach
Heart Chakra	Green	Heart, Lungs, Shoulder, Thymus
Throat Chakra	Blue	Neck, Spine, Thyroid
Third Eye Chakra	Purple	Ears, Eyes, Sinuses, Pineal, Pituitary
Crown Chakra	White or Gold	Brain, Hypothalamus

The chakras receive information through vibrations and respond only to the information to which they are tuned, allowing all the rest to pass. This information is of the emotional and spiritual realm, and cannot be seen by the human eye. When a chakra intercepts energy of similar vibration, it responds by taking the energy into the body, acting effectively like a transformer: It links various aspects of the physical body to its non-physical counterparts. Negative energy that enters the chakras can manifest in the body as disease and psychological or spiritual problems. Balancing the chakras is a way to prevent negative energy from damaging the body.

Every second of every day, the chakra system is processing information, determining what is useful, and storing it in its place in your mind, body, or spirit. So, you can quickly see why an out-of-tune chakra could cause potential problems. Like a radio, if the signal isn't clear and on the right frequency, all you get is static!

While all chakras respond to energy, only the Root, Solar Plexus, and Crown chakras are able to access and receive energies from the Higher Power, also known as the universal consciousness. Any other chakra can receive these energies only after they have been filtered through one of these three. Energy naturally moves within the chakra system. However, energy movement through the chakras can be facilitated by yoga, meditation, and the stimulation of chakra areas by massage, reiki (therapeutic touch), and of course, reflexology!

WHAT'S THE PURPOSE OF THE CHAKRA SYSTEM?

The purpose of the chakra system is to bring the body into a higher frequency of vibration in order to purify and heal any negative energy lodged therein. In many Eastern spiritual traditions, illness is seen as a depletion of one's internal power, or spirit. Therefore, by strengthening your internal power, you can resist disease and help your body to heal naturally. Similar to reflexology, in which all disease is regarded as an imbalance of energy in the body, the chakras provide an innate system for balancing energy and enhancing your health. What's more, through the chakra system your spirit and soul can become receptive to and communicate with greater cosmic powers.

If you're experiencing physical, emotional, or spiritual problems, you may have an imbalance in one or more of the chakra centers. If you're sensitive to the energy around you, sometimes you can even sense when someone close to you has a chakra imbalance. You may feel that the person in literally sucking the energy from you. And in some ways, they are! Since their chakra system is out of balance, they are energetically pulling energy from your own chakra centers. If you're ever in this situation, you can protect yourself by imaging a white light surrounding your entire body and shielding your energy from others.

In order to figure out which chakra is out of balance, all you have to do is recognize which mental and emotional issues, and which physical dysfunctions, correspond to which chakra. Then, you can move on to working that chakra point (or several points) in your feet!

THE ELEMENTS

In Chinese medicine, it is believed that our bodies are composed of five elements: wood, fire, earth, metal, and water. Each element corresponds to particular organs, emotions, seasons, colors, and other characteristics. Just as every organ is associated with a specific chakra, every organ is also associated with one of the five elements. Every organ also corresponds to a specific energy, either yin (negative) energy or yang (positive) energy. The Chinese believe that for good health and longevity, you must be aligned with nature and live harmoniously with all five elements and all living beings. If there is an imbalance of energy and you are not in tune with one of the five elements, disease can manifest in the associated part of the body. By attuning yourself to the five elemental energies, you can learn to balance your energy, heal your body, and prevent disease.

Reflexology helps the flow of energy through the body and improves the balance of the five elements. It isn't difficult to combine reflexology with the elements. For example, if you have a problem that corresponds with the Root chakra, you could choose a very earthy-scented oil like patchouli and rub it into that reflex spot. This supports the earth energy in that chakra and gives you smooth skin with which to work at the same time! An alternative way of bringing the elements to bear is surrounding yourself with them while you're working your feet. For example, it makes sense to sit down on the ground and connect with "earth," or Root chakra, while you perform reflexology. In cases where direct connection isn't possible, place representative items of that element in the room where you generally work your feet, like a cup of water and sea shells near you when stimulating the second chakra reflex point.

TUNE UP THE CHAKRAS THROUGH YOUR FEET

Every reflex point on your feet has a corresponding chakra. In the following pages, you'll find descriptions of the seven chakras, along with the reflex area with which they correspond and the problems that may indicate that the chakra is out of balance. If you identify with any of the mental and emotional issues, or with the physical problems, concentrate on stimulating that area to send healing energy to that chakra. You can do this by using reflexology thumb-pressure techniques on the reflex area, or simply by focusing your mind on the color associated with that particular chakra and visualizing that color filling either the chakra or the reflex point on the foot. Another approach is combining color therapy with reflexology by wearing the color of the out-of-balance chakra as you work your feet. This surrounds you with the best possible vibrations for the work at hand.

An all-over chakra tune-up can be done by stimulating your entire foot through reflexology, following the natural progression of the chakras from the base to the head. Alternatively, try closing your eyes and imaging swirling balls of color deep within your body. Beginning with the color red at the base of the spine, imagine the colors of the rainbow appearing, one at a time and in order. Move up your spine a few inches and focus on the next color, orange. And the next, and the next, until you reach purple, then white, at the top of your head. As you move toward the head, imagine pulling the energy from each chakra upward, from the base of the spine to the top of the head. This easy visualization technique can help you move energy up the chakra system and can balance the chakras that need support. It is also a useful visualization to try while working the reflex points, moving the visualization along as you move to new points on the foot!

By giving your chakras a "tune-up," you can strengthen your body and soul at the same time. And don't wait until you become ill before you attend to the health of your energy system. Get to know your inner feelings, learn to feel when your energy centers are out of balance, and take the steps that are necessary to heal yourself at the energy level.

Part II:
The Chakras, Your Sole, and Your Soul

Chakra 1: Root chakra

Color: Red

Location: At the base of the spine

Element: Earth

Associated Organs: Physical body support, base of spine, legs, bones, feet, rectum, immune system

Areas on Reflexology Sox™: Colon, hemorrhoids, spine

What is it?

The Root chakra, sometimes referred to as the "Muladhara chakra" in Tantric literature, is the first of the energy centers and it's related to grounding, rooting, and support. It is associated with interconnection with the earth, reincarnation, past lives, and repeated physical embodiment. The Root chakra is related to our levels of physical energy, and the will to live in physical reality.

One of the roles of the Root chakra is to transform and refine energy before it enters the higher chakra centers. Kundalini energy, which is sexual-spirited energy, is stored in this chakra and can be activated through yoga to rise through each of the chakras and up through the top of the head to the Crown chakra. As this happens, spiritual growth and awareness of other levels of energy and perceptions occur.

How it affects you

When the Root chakra is open and functioning well, one has a powerful will to live, is full of physical energy, vitality, and potency. When it's weak, blocked, or closed, most of one's physical vitality is blocked, and the person does not present a strong physical impression. A person who suffers from a weak or blocked Root chakra will lack physical power and coordination, will avoid physical activity, may find it difficult to express themselves physically, and will probably have a weak or sickly constitution. This person may even feel invisible.

Since this chakra is related to grounding, a blocked Root chakra may make you feel like you don't have your feet on the ground, that you don't have a firm foundation, and that you're up in the clouds. On the other hand, if the Root chakra is overactive, the person may depend on immediate external stimuli. These are the people who are constantly looking for something to do, somewhere to go. They are not content to just be at home and stay in one place. Alternatively, they may become fixated on security-related issues and unable to focus on anything else.

If the Root chakra is active but malfunctioning, the person may tend towards physical violence. This is usually someone who has no sense of law and order and no understanding of belonging to a community or to society in general. Typically, they have no family support and are often loners.

Associated physical problems

Chronic lower back pain

Sciatica

Varicose veins

Colon cancer/problems

Depression

Immunity-related problems

Associated emotional and spiritual concerns

Physical family and group safety and security

Ability to provide for life's requirements

Ability to stand up for oneself

Feeling grounded and at home

Social and familial law and order

Physical expression

CHAKRA 2: LOWER ABDOMEN CHAKRA

Color: Orange

Location: Just above the genital area

Element: Water

Associated Organs: Sexual organs, large intestine, lower vertebrae, pelvis, appendix,
bladder, hips

Areas on Reflexology Sox™: Bladder, hips, sciatica, sex organs, small intestine, urinary tract

What is it?

The Lower Abdomen chakra is the center for sexual energy, creativity, and pure emotion. This chakra processes *prana* (oxygen) from the atmosphere and transforms it into an energy that is used for sexuality, creativity, spiritual awareness, and integration. It is associated with water and has a foundation based on raw energy and power.

How it affects you

When the Lower Abdominal chakra is open, a person has a lot of sexual energy and sexual power, as well as a lot of energy and healing energy. People who have an open second chakra are often very creative and involved in the arts. They are often free spirits, who are comfortable with their sexuality and their place in relationships.

When this chakra is blocked, sexual sensations will be weak and disappointing and the person may have low self-esteem. People who have problems with guilt and sin, especially in the religious sense (i.e. the body is sinful or sex is dirty) may have problems with this chakra. They may also have issues with money, in that they feel unworthy of spending money on themselves.

If this chakra is overactive, the result may be excessive or uncontrolled sexual energy, even nymphomania. People with overactive second chakras may also be control freaks who are extremely focused on money and the acquisition of material things.

Associated physical problems

Chronic lower back pain

Sciatica

Gynecological problems

Pelvic pain

Sexual potency

Urinary problems

Associated emotional and spiritual concerns

Creativity

Power and control

Money and sex

Blame and guilt

Respect in relationships

CHAKRA 3: SOLAR PLEXUS CHAKRA

Color: Yellow

Location: In the center of the body

Element: Fire

Associated Organs: Abdomen, stomach, upper intestines, liver, gallbladder, kidney, pancreas, adrenal glands, spleen, middle spine

Areas on Reflexology Sox™: Adrenals, kidneys, liver, solar plexus, spleen, stomach

What is it?

The Solar Plexus chakra, located in the center of the body, is a very important chakra because it relates to our personal will power, metabolic energy, intention, and integrity. This chakra represents the male, creative, yang energy in the body. It brings to us our desires and impulses, and controls our emotions and physical power. This chakra is where feeling and being are assimilated. Associated with the element of fire, it is the foundation of our individual essence or personality.

How it affects you

The Solar Plexus chakra provides "gut feeling" reactions or "psychic impressions." It can bring us joy, sadness, inspired reactions, and heightened emotions. This chakra stimulates the sympathetic nervous system, which prepares the body for activity by producing adrenaline. When it is open and balanced, you have a sense of wholeness, gentleness, and inner peace, together with a great deal of emotional strength. You are independent, self-reliant, responsible, and courageous. A balanced Solar Plexus chakra strengthens you by supporting and reinforcing personal power and motivation.

When it's out of balance or holding negative energy, this chakra can cause unhealthy thoughts and actions. It may lead to anxiety and panic attacks. If it is blocked, you may feel weak, insecure, and easily swayed by others. You are easily intimidated and scared to make any decisions by yourself (possibly turning into a proverbial wallflower). If this chakra is overactive, it may cause you to be excessively forceful, pushing your will onto others. People with overactive third chakras can be aggressive, bossy, dominating, self-centered, and narcissistic.

Associated Physical Problems:

Arthritis

Gastric or duodenal ulcers

Colon/intestinal problems

Pancreatitis/diabetes

Indigestion

Eating disorders

Liver dysfunction

Hepatitis

Adrenal problems

Associated emotional and spiritual concerns

Trust

Fear and intimidation

Self-esteem, self-confidence, and self-respect

Self-care and care of others

Responsibility for making decisions

Sensitivity to criticism

Personal honor

Authority issues

CHAKRA 4: HEART CHAKRA

Color: Green

Location: In the center of the chest, two to three inches above the solar plexus

Element: Air

Associated Organs: Heart and circulatory system, lungs, shoulders and arms, ribs/breasts, diaphragm, thymus gland

Areas on Reflexology Sox™: Heart, lungs, shoulder, thymus

What is it?

The Heart chakra is the center of love, compassion, relationships, and associations. It's also related to other virtuous emotions, such as joy, happiness, honesty, respect, and generosity, and with loving oneself in a sincere, non-egotistical way. This is probably why in so many cultures the heart is said to be the seat of the soul. This chakra also helps us connect with those we love.

Associated with the element air, the heart chakra controls the circulation of blood and vitalizes the life stream. It is believed that "the heart is the mother in all of us," because it teaches lessons of kindness, forgiveness, love, peace, and harmony along with laughter and playfulness. The heart is where lessons of unconditional love and self-acceptance guide us to higher levels of being and loving. Through the Heart chakra we can feel a connection and sense of oneness with others, the world, and the Divine.

How it affects you

When the Heart chakra is open, it becomes the channel for universal love, and it generates the virtues of the heart through the whole body. The Heart chakra is very important in spiritual healing. When it's open it can remove fear and bring compassion in the form of spiritual love, which is a powerful tool in the quest for wholeness.

All the energies metabolized through the chakras travel up the center of the body and into the heart chakra, before moving out through the hands or eyes of the healer. Once the heart opens, the Higher Self is able to work through this center. People who have opened their Heart chakra are usually happy and peaceful. They can nurture strong relationships with others because they have learned the values of forgiveness and compassion. These people generally have less stress in their lives and may even live longer.

However, when there is an insufficient flow of love or emotional nourishment to the Heart chakra, it becomes blocked or even closed. Then, negative emotions such as hatred, guilt, self-ishness, paranoia, impatience, and self-pity can emerge. With a closed heart, one is unable to feel love for anyone, including oneself; any self-love becomes twisted and narcissistic. These people go through life with scowls on their faces and tension in every part of their bodies. They cannot let go of resentment and anger, so they keep it inside. Eventually, these negative emotions manifest as disease.

Associated physical problems

Heart problems

Asthma

Allergies

Lung cancer

Bronchial problems

Upper back and shoulder problems

Breast cancer

Associated emotional and spiritual concerns

Love and hatred

Forgiveness and compassion

Hope and trust

Resentment and bitterness

Grief and anger

Self-centeredness

Self abuse

Loneliness and commitment

CHAKRA 5: THROAT CHAKRA

Color: Blue

Location: In the throat, between the collarbones

Element: Sound

Associated Organs: Throat, thyroid, trachea, neck vertebrae, mouth, teeth and gums,
esophagus, parathyroid, hypothalamus

Areas on Reflexology Sox™: Neck, spine, thyroid

What is it?

The Throat chakra is related to communication, self-expression, and creativity. It is the Mother chakra, which begins the three yin or female energy chakras of the body. Associated with the element of sound, the Throat chakra rules the faculty of speech. It is also associated with clairaudience (hearing spiritual voices), and with our reception of sounds, words, music, tastes, and smells. The Throat chakra is your voice, communicating concrete thoughts that are received from the solar plexus. The voice represents your "intent," and it can inflict pain or kindness. The Throat chakra also works in tandem with the heart chakra in the front of the body to activate happiness, peace, love, and joy.

This chakra can focus and direct our thoughts into words. Since all life experiences come directly from our thoughts, then words, then actions, the voice has great power in transforming intentions and desires, and realizing our dreams. In a sense, this center acts as a pump that sends energy to higher centers. The Throat chakra is the center of the ego-self and will-power. It is the center from which we transform thought into word and deed in the external physical world. Another function associated with this chakra is the absorption of physical and emotional nourishment. This can manifest as sensuous desire and enjoyment of food.

How it affects you

When the Throat chakra is open, there is feeling of freedom and a deep sense of the meaning of life and the universe—an awareness that one's will is in harmony with Divine will. When this center is open and functioning well, you're able to embrace others with love and warmth. It is easy to express yourself and your speech is clear and smooth. You are secure in your personal expression so you can make decisions and pursue your goals in life with little hesitation.

When the Throat chakra is blocked, there may be a lack of will power and motivation. You may feel burdened, hopeless, inadequate, and melancholy. You may find it difficult to speak or even get the right words out, but at the same time, you may be stubborn and unwilling to change. Often, people who are blocked in this chakra are very shy and cannot find the strength to communicate their feelings and thoughts. They hold things inside and cannot express their emotions. To compensate for this inability to communicate what's going on inside, people with blocked Throat chakras may compulsively eat or develop other eating disorders, such as bulimia and anorexia.

When this center is overactive, the result may lead to immoral, irresponsible behavior. People may be overly expressive to the point of being obnoxious. They need you to hear them, so they are loud and often offensive. They also tend to overreact to everything with great drama, jump into situations with little forethought, and become self-proclaimed experts in every conversation.

Associated physical problems

Throat problems (laryngitis)

Mouth/gum problems

Scoliosis

Swollen glands

Thyroid problems

Associated emotional and spiritual concerns

Personal expression

Choice and strength of will

Following dreams

Using personal power to create

Addiction

Judgment and criticism

Faith and knowledge

Capacity to make decisions

CHAKRA 6: THIRD EYE CHAKRA

Color: Purple

Location: Between the eyes

Element: Light

Associated Organs: Brain, nervous system, eyes, ears, nose, pineal and pituitary glands

Areas on Reflexology Sox™: Ears, eyes, sinuses, pineal, pituitary

What is it?

The Third Eye chakra is related to intuition, perception, and the imagination. Associated with the element of light, it is the energy center where you can perceive higher spiritual planes. The Third Eye helps you to see all circumstances around you, and it's the key to wisdom, knowledge, and truth. While dreaming, meditating, or working the chakra energies, there may be colors, pictures, feelings, and inner knowledge that come to you through the Third Eye. When this occurs, this energy center gives you the capacity to visualize and understand mental concepts. This chakra is the ultimate power center for perceiving and healing yourself and others.

How it affects you

If the Third Eye chakra is open and balanced, you may be very imaginative, intuitive, and creative. You may have psychic abilities and be able to see, feel, or know things that other people, whose Third Eye is less developed, may not. If this chakra is more developed than other centers, you may have difficulty relating to the everyday routine and physical matters, and will be too much "in the clouds." Similarly, if this chakra is strong but malfunctioning, you may tend to get caught up in illusion and glamour and use drugs that temporarily provide that fantasy world.

On the other hand, if this center is blocked or closed, you may have a very limited, unimaginative consciousness, and will tend to live life in a little box, with no higher guidance or inspiration. You may reject all spiritual aspects and intuition, and only believe in science, intellect, and surface meanings. People with a blocked Third Eye refuse to open their eyes and mind to anything that is not concrete and proven. They are usually not religious and often do not believe in God, reincarnation, or life after death.

Associated physical problems

Brain problems
Neurological disturbances
Blindness and deafness
Spinal problems
Learning disabilities
Seizures

Associated emotional and spiritual concerns

Truth
Self-evaluation
Intellectual abilities
Feelings of inadequacy
Openness to new ideas
Ability to learn from experience
Emotional intelligence
Faith

CHAKRA 7: CROWN CHAKRA

Color: White or Gold

Location: At the top and center of the head

Element: Thought

Associated Organs: Muscular system, skeletal system, skin

Areas on Reflexology Sox™: Brain

What is it?

The Crown chakra is the basis of knowledge, information, and understanding. Associated with thought, it's connected to the pineal gland, which regulates the body's internal clock and was considered by the philosopher Descartes to be the link between the body and the soul. In keeping with this idea, Eastern mysticism teaches that the Crown chakra connects directly to our Higher Self and it brings reverence, knowledge of infinity, and insights from this spiritual understanding. This is the center through which you can connect to planes of consciousness beyond and above the individual self and "concrete" reality. Through it you can literally reach the heavens or other energy realms, and you can receive revelations from higher planes of existence. These revelations are the source of genius intelligence, higher intuition, and religious experiences.

Through the Crown chakra, it is believed that you can rise through the center of your head and project healing and pure, unconditional love energies anywhere in the universe. This is the basis for "energy-based" therapies such as reiki and therapeutic touch, as well as the "power of prayer." This chakra also relates to immortality, angels, grace, interaction with Divine forces, and self-realization.

How it affects you

When the Crown Center is open, spirituality is inherent and you are automatically drawn to mystical or sacred teachings. You may possess an inner knowledge of a higher, universal level of consciousness and you may have the ability to see auras, receive guidance from higher forces, and feel bliss. Or you may simply have an intrinsic understanding of truth and purpose. People with open Crown chakras are often psychic, and are sometimes referred to as "old souls." They can see beyond the concrete to the truth.

On the other hand, when this center is blocked, all senses of spirituality and creativity, which ultimately come from above, are also blocked. You may have a very narrow, limited consciousness, and focus on the material world. If the Crown chakra is out of balance, it can cause you to be unable to imagine anything beyond this world. You may refuse to let go of fear and anxiety, and be depressed and unsatisfied. You may question the meaning of life and wonder about the point of it all.

Associated physical problems

Energy problems

Depression

Chronic fatigue (not linked to physical problems)

Extreme sensitivity to light, sound, and other environmental factors

Associated emotional and spiritual concerns

Ability to trust life

Values, ethics, and courage

Humanitarianism

Selflessness

Belief and inspiration

Spirituality and devotion

Balancing and Healing the Body, Mind, and Spirit

Stimulating the chakras through reflexology is a powerful way to balance the energy in the body, heal congested areas, and prevent future illnesses from developing. The body, mind, and spirit are interconnected and they come together through the chakra system. By "tuning-up" your chakras, you can heal your body on an energetic level. This will not only improve your physical well-being, but also can promote greater self-awareness and nurture spiritual growth. It's remarkable yet true: By combining reflexology, chakra balancing, color therapy, and the ancient principles of Chinese medicine, you can improve the health of your energy system and strengthen your body, mind, and soul at the same time... all through your feet!

Appendix:
Foot Facts and
Suggested
Further Reading

REFLEXOLOGY ASSOCIATIONS AND WEBSITES

If you are interested in learning more about reflexology, there are many great schools that offer comprehensive reflexology classes, as well as reflexologist referral information. To find a school in your area, contact either the international organization or one of the state associations listed below.

Currently, there is no nationally recognized license to practice reflexology and reflexology is not recognized as a separate modality of treatment from massage therapy. Therefore, in most states there are no laws governing the practice of reflexology. The only qualification that may be required is that you have a license to practice massage therapy. Before you open up a reflexology practice, the best thing to do is to contact your state organization and find out what laws are in effect where you live and explain that you would like to set up a practice.

For information on classes, seminars, and educational materials, contact:

The International Institute of Reflexology (The Original Ingham Method of Reflexology)
P.O. Box 12642
St. Petersburg, FL 33733-2642
Tel: (727) 343.4811
Fax: (727) 381.2807

Modern Institute of Reflexology
7063 West Colfax Avenue
Denver, CO 80215
Tel: (303) 237.1562
Toll-free: (800) 533.1837
Fax: (303) 237.1606
e-mail: footdocs@ix.netcom.com

For information on the voluntary national reflexology certification program as well as certified reflexologist referrals, contact:

American Reflexology Certification Board
P.O. Box 620607
Littleton, CO 80162
Tel: (303) 933.6921
Fax: (303) 904-0460

NATIONAL ASSOCIATION

Reflexology Association of America (RAA)
4012 South Rainbow Ste. K-PMB# K585
Las Vegas, NV 89103-2059
Tel: (702) 871.9522

INTERNATIONAL ORGANIZATIONS

International Council of Reflexologists (ICR)
P.O. Box 621963
Littleton, CO 80162
(303) 627.4052
e-mail: interncouncilreflex@juno.com

REFLEXOLOGY ASSOCIATION OF CANADA

On the web, visit: http://reflexologycanada.ca

REFLEXOLOGY WEB SITES

http://www.basicknead.com
   Basic Knead is the massage therapy company founded by author Michelle Kluck. This website offers information on reflexology and on the latest reflexology and massage therapy products and instructional videos produced by Kluck.

http://www.reflexology-usa.org
   The International Institute of Reflexology features information on the Original Ingham Method of Reflexology, seminars, classes, certification programs, books, and local reflexologist referrals.

http://www.positivehealth.com
   Positive Health is the UK's definitive magazine in Complementary Medicine, with features covering all therapies including acupuncture, aromatherapy, asthma, herbal and Chinese medicine, homoeopathy, massage, nutrition, reflexology, yoga, and zero balancing.

www.ahha.org
   American Holistic Health Association. A leading national resource connecting people with vital solutions for reaching a higher level of wellness. Offers database of holistic practitioners and more.

www.healthcalendar.com
   The Global Health Calendar features leading events in the fields of health care, natural therapies, fitness, medicine, environment, etc.

STATE ASSOCIATIONS

Alabama

Alabama Reflexology Association (ARA)
P.O. Box 4715
Huntsville, AL 35815

California

Reflexology Association of California (RAC)
P.O. Box 641156
Los Angeles, CA 90064
www.reflexcal.org

Foot Reflexology Awareness Association
(FRAA)
P.O. Box 7622
Mission Hills, CA 91346

Colorado

Associated Reflexologists of Colorado (ARC)
P.O. Box 697
Englewood, CO 80151

Florida

Florida Association of Reflexology (FAR)
235 31st Street N.
St. Petersburg, FL 33713

Georgia

Georgia Reflexology Association (GRA)
2206 Huntingdon Chase
Atlanta, GA 30350

Illinois

Reflexology Association of Illinois (RAI)
P.O. Box 5515
Buffalo Grove, IL 60089-5515

Massachusetts

New England Association of Reflexology
(N.E.A.R.)
P.O. Box 1718
Onset, MA 02558
e-mail: vvoner1357@aol.com

Maine

Maine Council of Reflexologists (MCR)
5 Washington Street #9
Brewer, ME 04412

Minnesota

Reflexology of Minnesota (ROM)
P.O. Box 662
Hinckley, MN 55037

New Jersey

Reflexology Association of New Jersey (RANJ)
187 Whitehead Avenue
South River, NJ 08882

New Mexico

Professional Association of Reflexologists of
New Mexico
P.O. Box 27292
Albuquerque, NM 87125-7292
e-mail: ftreflex2@aol.com

New York

New York State Reflexology Association
(NYRA)
6 Willow Ridge Lane
Lancaster, NY 14086
Tel: (716) 656.0425
Fax: (716) 656.9303
e-mail: ReflexManRep@Juno.com

Nevada

Nevada Reflexology Organization (NRO)
P.O. Box 27108
Las Vegas, NV 89126-1108
Tel: (702) 615.3332
url:www.nvreflexology.org
e-mail: NRO@wizard.com

North Dakota

North Dakota Reflexology Association (NDRA)
1413 N. 19th Street
Bismarck, ND 58501

Ohio

Ohio Association of Reflexologists
32945 Detroit Road
Avon, Ohio 44011-2017
Tel: (440) 937.5580

Oregon

Oregon Association of Reflexology (OAR)
2291 Jubilant Avenue
Medford, OR 97504
Tel/Fax: (541) 858.0133
e-mail: ktreflex@medford.com

Pennsylvania

Pennsylvania Reflexology Association (PRA)
P.O. Box 796
Glenside, PA 19038

Washington

Washington Reflexology Association
P.O. Box 1944
Edmonds, WA 98020-1944
Tel: (425) 771.9572

Wisconsin

Reflexology Organization of Wisconsin (ROW)
904 Gail Place
Fort Atkinson, WI 53538

Dwight C. Byers, *Better Health With Foot Reflexology* (St. Petersburg, FL: Ingham Publishing, Inc., 1991). This book, written by the nephew of Eunice Ingham, describes the Original Ingham Method of Reflexology and includes charts of the reflex areas in the hands and feet. It is an important reference guide for those who want to learn more about reflexology.

Eunice Ingham, *The Original Works of Eunice D. Ingham: Stories the Feet Can Tell Thru Reflexology, Stories the Feet Have Told Thru Reflexology* (St. Petersburg, FL: Ingham Publishing, Inc., 1984). This book was written by the founder of reflexology and revised by her nephew, Dwight C. Byers. It is a remarkable story about her work in developing modern reflexology.

Harry Bond Bressler, *Zone Therapy* (Mokelumne Hill, CA: Health Research, 1971). This book gives details on the development and principles behind zone therapy.

Laura Norman, *Feet First* (New York: Simon & Schuster, 1988). This book is an excellent guide to understanding reflexology. If you're interested in becoming a reflexologist, this book offers information on techniques and practical applications.

Mildred Carter and Tammy Weber, *Body Reflexology: Healing At Your Fingertips* (New York: Parker Publishing Company, 1994). If you're interested in learning about reflexology for the whole body, this book gives information on how to combine foot, hand, and ear reflexology to improve your health.

Thomas Claire, *Bodywork: What Type of Massage to Get— And How To Make The Most of It* (New York: William Morrow and Company, Inc., 1995). If you're interested in learning more about bodywork in general, this is the book for you. This book gives essential information about almost every kind of bodywork, including reflexology.

VIDEOS TO VIEW

Living Arts Massage Practice: Reflexology. This award-winning instructional video teaches reflexology techniques and explains exactly how to give a great reflexology treatment.

Living Arts Massage Practice: Couples Massage. This video teaches couples how to give each other a therapeutic massage, including a very effective reflexology treatment.

Living Arts Massage Practice: Infant Massage. This video teaches the techniques of baby massage, including how to use reflexology on babies.

Living Arts Massage Practice: Acupressure. This video explains and teaches the techniques of acupressure.

Living Arts Massage Practice: Pregnancy. This video teaches easy-to-learn techniques to help relieve the common discomforts associated with pregnancy. It includes a section on how to give an effective and extremely relaxing foot treatment.

Living Arts Massage Practice: Therapeutic Touch. This video teaches the ancient practice of balancing the open energy system in and around the body. It can help you understand the concepts of how energy moves through the body.

All of these videos are available at most Borders bookstores, or can be ordered by calling Living Arts at 1.800.254.8464 or visiting www.livingartsonline.com.

To order reflexology and other massage products (such as lotions, essential oils, and charts), contact:

The Bodywork Emporium
414 Broadway
Santa Monica, CA 90401
Tel: (310) 394.4475
Toll free: (800) TABLE-4U
www.bodyworkemporium.com